I0120015

BIOANTHROPOLOGY

THE BASICS

Bioanthropology: The Basics offers an engaging and accessible introduction to the science of biological anthropology, exploring human origins, evolution, and the biological dimensions of what it means to be human. Through illuminating examples and case studies, this comprehensive text guides readers through essential topics while connecting our evolutionary past to contemporary discussions about human variation. Topics covered include:

- Human origins
- DNA
- Primates
- Evolution

Bioanthropology: The Basics is ideal for undergraduate students approaching biological anthropology for the first time, scholars from other disciplines seeking cross-disciplinary insights, and general readers curious about human origins and the scientific study of what makes us human.

Marc Kissel is Associate Professor of Anthropology at Appalachian State University, USA.

THE BASICS SERIES

The Basics is a highly successful series of accessible guidebooks which provide an overview of the fundamental principles of a subject area in a jargon-free and undaunting format.

Intended for students approaching a subject for the first time, the books both introduce the essentials of a subject and provide an ideal springboard for further study. With over 50 titles spanning subjects from artificial intelligence (AI) to women's studies, *The Basics* are an ideal starting point for students seeking to understand a subject area.

Each text comes with recommendations for further study and gradually introduces the complexities and nuances within a subject.

BUSINESS START-UP
ALEXANDRINA PAUCEANU

ACTING HEIGHTENED TEXT
CATHERINE WEIDNER

LIBERTARIANISM
JESSICA FLANIGAN AND CHRISTOPHER FREIMAN

CLOSE READING (SECOND EDITION)
DAVID GREENHAM

FEMINISM
RENEE HEBERLE

MINDFULNESS
SOPHIE SANSOM, DAVID SHANNON, AND TARAVAJRA

URBAN DESIGN
TIM HEATH AND FLORIAN WIEDMANN

PUBLIC RELATIONS (SECOND EDITION)
DEBORAH SILVERMAN

EDUCATION STUDIES
CATHERINE SIMON

DRAG
MARK EDWARD AND CHRIS GREENOUGH#

BIOANTHROPOLOGY
MARC KISSEL

For more information about this series, please visit: www.routledge.com/ The-Basics/book-series/B

BIOANTHROPOLOGY

THE BASICS

Marc Kissel

Routledge
Taylor & Francis Group
NEW YORK AND LONDON

Designed cover image: Veronika Oliinyk via Getty Images

First published 2026
by Routledge
605 Third Avenue, New York, NY 10158

and by Routledge
4 Park Square, Milton Park, Abingdon, Oxon, OX14 4RN

Routledge is an imprint of the Taylor & Francis Group, an informa business

ISBN: 9781032487229 (hbk)
ISBN: 9781032487236 (pbk)
ISBN: 9781003390442 (ebk)

DOI: 10.4324/9781003390442

Typeset in Bembo
by Deanta Global Publishing Services, Chennai, India

CONTENTS

LIST OF FIGURES

LIST OF TABLES

ACKNOWLEGEMENTS

My first anthropology class was an archaeology course taught by Dr. Pam Crabtree. I can never thank her enough for the world she opened up to me. I also owe my career to my Ph.D adviser John Hawks, who took me in as a wayward grad student. My postdoc mentor Agustin Fuentes never fails to keep me optimistic and in awe. When I grow up, I hope to be like him.

Meagan Simpson, my editor at Routledge Anthropology, is simply the best. When she approached me with the idea of writing something for the Basic Series I was intimidated by the idea but her kindness and compassion helped make this project real (especially when things went sideways and I needed more time). Production editor Megan Hiatt kept me on track for the last few months. Likewise, Hamish Ironside painstakingly checked the whole manuscript for consistency, correct spelling, and grammatical mistakes and typographical errors (of course, any remaining errors are mine!).

My colleagues at Appalachian State University (the real ASU!) were supportive and always willing to chat. I'm grateful for a summer stipend the university gave me to help finish this book. Susan Lappan, Sophie Dent, Krista Lewis, and Anna Brown, among others, gave useful feedback and advice, even if they don't all agree that marmosets are the best primate.

Various students and colleagues gave feedback, comments, and support. Piper Voakes reminded me that to not include *Homo floresiensis* would be a bad move. Sarah Harrison, Maggie Mason, Kenna Wadlington, Ria Klausmeyer, and so many others were helpful as well in various classes. Jenni French, Somaye Khaksar, Leon Levine, Anne Belk, team MMM, and so many others helped me get this over the finish line

My mother wanted to be an anthropologist/archaeologist, and although she never had the chance, she did open the niche so I could become an anthropologist. My wife Jenna has moved more times than anyone should. I am very lucky to have her in my life and she should get coauthorship on anything I do (plus she is a librarian so that makes her even more amazing). Thanks for all you do. My kids Harper and Sutton have put up with a father who has a weird job, keeps odd hours, and is stranger than most of the dads they know (at least, that is what they tell me). They also make sure I stay somewhat up on pop culture so that my students don't think I'm totally out of touch.

INTRODUCTION

Many of us, especially as we get older, find ourselves wanting to know more about our ancestors. Numerous people invest time tracing their lineage and countless people spend money for services that help to create their family tree. We are often fascinated to learn who are ancestors were, especially if they turn out to be famous.

While there are many companies that can help you create your own family tree, my job is to tell people about their *much more distant* relatives. My colleagues and I try to untangle the processes by which our species, *Homo sapiens*, became fully human. That is a story that is both fascinating and always changing. One of the main goals of this book is to let you know the scientific understanding of our origins.

But before we get into why this book was written I want to first tell you about something that happened almost 100 years ago, when the world's leading expert in artificial insemination became curious about just how different we are from chimpanzees, our closest living relatives.

In September of 1928 the Russian scientist Il'ya Ivanovich Ivanov (1870–1932) wrote to Rosalia Abreu (1862–1930), a very wealthy animal lover who lived in Cuba. He asked her if she could

DOI: 10.4324/9781003390442-1

help him with his plan to create a human–ape hybrid (In the early part of the twentieth century not much was known about how reproduction worked. Since chimps are the closest living relatives of humans, Ivanov thought this kind of hybrid would be viable.) As one of the leading experts in captive primates (she may have been the first person to have a chimp give birth in captivity) Abreu was the perfect person to address his question.

Abreu originally thought it was a great idea. However, she became nervous that the news of such an experiment at her zoo would cause problems for her and attract the wrong kind of attention to her work. In her will, though, she wrote that 'No cross of female chimpanzee with man. Man is too big and, if the cross should be successful, the childbirth would be too painful for the mother. No objection to cross of male chimpanzee with female *Homo*.'

As an anthropologist who specializes in the study of human origins, I have received different versions of the human–chimp baby question. While few people today would want to perform this experiment in real life, folks still wonder what would happen if a chimpanzee and a human did have a child. This has been asked by undergraduates in the classroom, airline passengers who notice the obscure article I am reading, or family members who are not really sure what I do for a living. While I do not normally tell complete strangers the story of this Russian scientist (who may have used his son's sperm in an earlier attempt to get a female chimpanzee pregnant …) I do often wonder why this question is so popular. While there are numerous ethical, moral, and technological reasons why this would not have worked, the larger question of why anyone would think this would be a good idea is left unasked. Based on how we treat people today who are a little different from us, I wonder if a human–chimp offspring would even be considered human and what rights the child would be given.

At its core I think the chimp–human hybrid question is really an examination about what it means to be human. Scientists, theologians, philosophers, novelists, poets, and others have discussed this idea for thousands of years. We now know that there is no single gene shared by all humans that is not found in other species that came before us. There is also no behavior that is distinctive and inclusive of all humans. Nor is it easy to find a morphological trait that exists only in contemporary *Homo sapiens* but is missing from other populations. Indeed, defining our species by what we have and what other species do not have has proved to be very difficult.

In this book I hope to convince you that what makes us human is our shared evolutionary history. This history is the one characteristic everyone reading this book has in common. It makes us distinct from the other primates such as chimps, gorillas, capuchins, baboons, and marmosets. It is a history that we have only begun to understand and one that we are always learning something new about.

Of course, humans have been telling stories about where we come from since the birth of storytelling. The fact that you and I share an ancestry that goes back at least 6 million years is a profound and remarkable fact, and something that is very important to reflect on and be aware of. That 6 million years of human history seems like a long time. But let's put that time into a geological perspective by imaging a timeline of Earth's history. Stretch your arms out to your sides and imagine that the tip of your left middle fingernail represents the formation of the planet Earth (about 4.5 billion years ago) and the tip of your right middle fingernail is today. If someone came along and trimmed your right fingernail, that bit of nail filings that lands on the floor would represent the length of time humans have been on the earth. In other words, our time on the planet has been fleeting. But in that relatively short time we have had an immense impact on the entire ecosystem.

To understand the processes by which we became human we need to rely on the science of biological anthropology.

Biological anthropology is a large tent. My colleagues study subjects such as the cold climate adaptations of reindeer herders, pregnancy and maternal health in American Samoa, immune response of getting tattoos, vocalizations of gibbons, the effects of climate change on humans in prehistory, why an earlier human species dragged their dead into a complex cave system, how a mother's milk helps her infants survive, and how we can use ancient DNA to understand behaviors of our extinct relatives. At its core, however, we are all interested in humans and their place in the world. We examine our own species through a framework of evolution and emphasize the intersection of biology and culture in human behavior.

This book is about how we can use biological anthropology to understand human origins. We will tour though the modern science of biological anthropology, discussing how the history of genetics is linked to the desire to keep secrets about what makes a sheep grow the best wool (Chapter 2), what the attempt to teach chimps sign language tells us about the origins of human language (Chapter 4), and how ancient bones let us know some incredible facts about what life was like millions of years ago (Chapter 5).

This book will also discuss *why* we study these topics as no one I know got in this for the money. For many anthropologists, the first reason is that it is interesting! We have the pleasure of studying something that many people like to read and learn about. And, as we will learn, biological anthropology can provide insight into the causes and consequences of human variation. To understand topics such as gender, sex, and race one needs to know a lot about what these variations came from.

Biological anthropology also helps us understand where we fit in the natural world. Humans are primates and much about our anatomy is a result of our primate heritage. For example, the slight involuntary movements of your arm or leg just as you are about to fall asleep may be a remnant of our evolutionary past. Our primate ancestors slept in trees and if their muscles started relaxing they could fall off the branch and hurt themselves. The involuntary contraction of the muscles helped to protect them from injury or death. But for most humans today it is just an annoying reflex that keeps us from falling asleep.

This book is also about how we came to learn about human biology and where the field is going. Many of the ideas presented in my first anthropology at the turn of the twenty-first century have been shown to be wrong. We now know that *Homo sapiens* are a hybrid of multiple different populations: Everyone reading this has genes from human populations that are no longer around, such as the Neandertals. After reading this book you will not only understand how we became human, but you will have a better way to talk about human variation in the present. As we will see, the processes by which we became human are more complicated than you may think and require knowledge from many different fields of study.

Chapter 1 discusses what anthropology as a whole is and how the various subfields of anthropology come together to create an integrated field that looks at humans as biocultural organisms. It also provides a short overview of the idea of evolution by natural selection, detailing how the past can be studied scientifically.

Chapter 2 is focused on genetics. In the last few decades, the use of DNA has changed a lot of what we know about human evolution. This chapter gives a framework for understanding the modern science of genomics, concentrating on the questions of how genes and the environment interact with each other. It also looks at how scientists today approach evolution at the micro level.

Chapter 3 is an overview of human biology, the branch of biological anthropology that examines traits such as skin color and other adaptations among, within, and between human populations to understand the origin and maintenance of these variables. This field is critical to understanding contemporary human variation and helps us push back on racist and sexist views.

Chapter 4 examines the nonhuman primates. As with other chapters in this book, it can only scratch the surface of the study of primatology. The chapter focuses on the adaptations of different primates to provide a view of what it means to be a primate and why humans are part of this group. Primatology is one of the most popular aspects of biological anthropology due to how interesting it is to learn about our close relative.

Chapter 5 is the first of two chapters the covers paleoanthropology, the study of human origins. This is split into two sections due to the amount of information that this covers. Chapter 5 looks at the earliest parts of human evolutionary history, from our split with our shared last common ancestor with chimpanzees to the earliest members of the genus *Homo*.

Chapter 6 summarizes the final periods of human evolution, looking at the origins of *Homo sapiens* and their interactions with other hominis. It also discusses how the origins of agriculture changed human biology and culture.

Finally, Chapter 7 touches on some final aspects of biological anthropology, looking at where the field is going and how it can have an impact on other aspects of human life.

A NOTE ON TERMINOLOGY

Anthropology in general is a way of rethinking how we view the world. One major lesson is that the language we use does not always reflect reality. Because of this we often need to update and change our terminology to reflect new knowledge. While science is a way of learning about the world that tries to be as objective as possible, true objectivity might be impossible since we all have biases.

A good example of this are how we think about biological sex. While it might seem obvious that there are only two sexes, as we talk about in Chapter 3 this is not the case. Scientists today have tried to find ways to center discussions about complex topics in ways that are more nuanced and to write more inclusively. At the same time, it can become confusing when terms we learned or were taught are no longer being used in the same way.

I try to avoid problematic terminology while also making the book as easy as possible to follow. In some instances, though, that might make the text a little confusing in places. But I think it is worth it. For example, the monkeys of the Americas are often called 'New World primates.' But the use of the word 'New' is somewhat colonialist. It erases and ignores the fact that Indigenous peoples were in the Americas for a much longer time than people of recent European descent. The taxonomic grouping that the monkeys in the Americas belong to is called the platyrrhines. This term, while useful, is not helpful outside of scientific discussions. In this book, I use platyrrhines or American monkeys, but note that even the latter has issues (the name has been taken from a European explorer). There is no good way to refer to this group that does not reflect some sort of historical perspective.

Another issue that biological anthropologists are currently grappling with is the use of human bones for academic research and teaching. Not all cultures feel it is appropriate for the remains of their ancestors to be studied and kept in museums or lab cabinets. Until recently, most biological anthropology students who took a human osteology course would learn skeletal anatomy from remains that were not obtained ethically. There is a movement in both medical schools and anthropology departments to only use bodies that were willed to be used for teaching purposes and to return or repatriate materials not ethically obtained.

Anthropology is often about making people question their core beliefs. It is also about learning to be comfortable with being uncomfortable.

FURTHER READING

Agarwal, Sabrina C. 2024. The Bioethics of Skeletal Anatomy Collections from India. *Nature Communications* 15(1): 1692. https://doi.org/10.1038/s41467-024-45738-6. *A recent overview of some of the ethical concerns in bioarcheology.*

Bezanson, Michelle, Liliana Cortés-Ortiz, Júlio César Bicca-Marques, Ramesh Boonratana, Susana Carvalho, Marina Cords, Stella De La Torre, et al. 2023. News and Perspectives: Words Matter in Primatology. *Primates* 65: 33–39. https://doi.org/10.1007/s10329-023-01104-6. *An overview of how primatologists have been thinking about the use of terms such as 'New World primates.'*

Carney, Scott. 2011. *The Red Market: On the Trail of the World's Organ Brokers, Bone Thieves, Blood Farmers, and Child Traffickers*. William Morrow. *An investigation into underworld where organs and bones are bought and sold, written by a journalist who also happens to be my roommate from graduate school.*

Rossiianov, Kirill. 2002. Beyond Species: Il'ya Ivanov and His Experiments on Cross Breeding Humans with Anthropoid Apes. *Science in Context* 15 (2): 277–316. https://doi.org/10.1017/S0269889702000455. *One of the best overviews of the work of Il'ya Ivanov and how his studies in hybridization were linked to larger issues of Russian politics and belief.*

1

WHAT IS BIOANTHROPOLOGY?

CHAPTER OVERVIEW

This chapter covers the history of bioanthropology (biological anthropology) as a field of study that seeks to understand humans from both a biological and a cultural perspective. In doing so, we will learn how we can scientifically understand the past and where the idea of evolution came from. After reading this section you will know not only what anthropology is but why it is important. You will also be able to contextualize the work that led to the understanding of where humans fit within the natural world. Finally, we will see how evolutionary thinking allows us to better understand where we come from and what it means to be human.

Another aim of this chapter is to reiterate the idea that science does not function within a vacuum. The scientists whose work we look at in this chapter are responding to the morale and politics of their day. Moreover, the idea of a lone genius acting on their own is inaccurate. As we will see, Charles Darwin, the scholar best associated with the idea of evolution, worked from previous scholarship and his contemporaries to formulate his views.

WHAT IS ANTHROPOLOGY?

Anthropology is a very wide-ranging discipline. In the American version, there are four subfields of anthropology: linguistic anthropology, cultural anthropology, archaeology, and bioanthropology (outside of the United States some of these fields might appear in different departments or research institutes). This section provides a brief overview of each of these fields. Importantly,

DOI: 10.4324/9781003390442-2

many anthropologists today think of themselves as doing integrative anthropology, a practice that reaches across the subfields and requires knowledge from all branches of anthropology.

Cultural anthropology (also known as sociocultural anthropology) studies aspects of contemporary human behavior through fieldwork and participant observation. This field is focused on how different cultures and groups organize themselves, asking people in different societies believe and think about their lives.

Many sociocultural anthropologists use **ethnography**, a distinctive fieldwork strategy of anthropology that entails field experience in another culture. Rather than reading about a group of people, a cultural anthropologist spends time with them and learns how they see the world. In some sense the goal of twentieth-century cultural anthropology was to learn the different ways people lived and to do so without assuming that there was a single correct way for people to act. Cultural anthropology is about becoming familiar with the unfamiliar and leaving our cultural biases behind.

As an example, the American anthropologist Margaret Mead (1901–1978) argued in her ethnography *Coming of Age in Samoa* that 'Romantic love as it occurs in [American] civilization, inextricably bound up with ideas of monogamy, exclusiveness, jealousy, and undeviating fidelity does not occur in Samoa.' Mead and others taught that the ideas, beliefs, and practices we learn as children and that we think are human universals are not in fact as wide-ranging as many tend to believe. Instead, it is our cultural background and ethnocentrism that makes us think that the way we live is the best way to live.

An important aspect of cultural anthropology is the idea that to fully know and understand another culture requires a knowledge of its members' beliefs and motivations. This idea is known as **cultural relativism**. In its most simple form, cultural relativism suggests that the context behind a behavior matters. For instance, the phrase 'I do wish we could chat longer, but I'm having an old friend for dinner' seems innocent enough when spoken by a coworker, but when spoken by the cannibal Hannibal Lecter in the movie *The Silence of the Lambs* it takes on a *very* different meaning.

Linguistic anthropology is the study of human speech and language. This field examines not just how we use language but how we are socialized through language. The ways in which we speak are affected by many factors. How we talk is also highly contextualized and politicized. Our word choices convey much about who we are.

In the United States many people refer to a basin that has a tap of running water for people to drink as a 'water fountain.' Others call it a 'drinking fountain.' And in some regions, it is called a 'bubbler.' What phrasing you use tends to indicate where you grew up. We will come across linguistic anthropology when we are thinking about the origins of symbolic thought and language.

Archaeology is the study of behaviors in the human past. Archaeologists reconstruct cultures in the past by looking at the material humans left behind, such as their tools or the trash from their meals. Archaeologists use the scientific method to examine **artifacts**, objects that has been made, used, or otherwise modified by human activity. These can be stone tools, copper axes, pottery shards, pieces of clothing, or anything else that someone has made. They also study **features**, culturally modified portions of the landscape such as postholes used in construction of a house or earthen mounds. **Ecofacts** are objects that provide information on the environment, such as animal bones, pollen grains, and plants. Finally, **sites** are places that exhibit evidence of human activity and are often made up of collections of artifacts, ecofacts, and/or features. Many biological anthropologists are trained as archaeologists, learning how to excavate and record data recovered from fieldwork.

Finally, in this text we are looking at **bioanthropology**, which studies *human biology within a framework of evolution and emphasizes the intersection between biology and culture*. Biological anthropologists need to be familiar with the other three fields, along with knowing about biology, genetics, and other sciences. It combines contemporary evolutionary theory with anthropological thought and ideas to understand and model human evolution.

As you can tell, anthropology encompasses a lot of different ways of thinking about humanity. Some anthropologists identify as scientists, while others are more focused on the humanities side of academia. Because of this, the American Anthropological Association conference has over 7,000 anthropologists talking about *very* different projects and ideas. But each of these subfields helps to answer the question of how to be human. While bioan-thropology focuses on the scientific interpretation of human biol-ogy and evolution, we need to keep in mind that we cannot create a wholly apolitical view of the past.

One important caveat is that the history given here is particular to American anthropology. The four fields of American anthro-pology represent different approaches to these questions. For that reason, biological anthropologists who were trained in American schools often have a different background than scholars from other countries. For example, archaeology is often housed in history or classics departments in the UK. Many biological anthropologists see themselves as integrative anthropologists, working across the subfields and using data generated within and outside of anthro-pology to fully explore questions of human origins and variation.

Anthropology is one of the most humanistic sciences (or, one of the most scientific of the humanities). Scholars who specialize in bioanthropology can often be trained to do lab work, excavate archaeological sites, collect biological data from living people, write statistical code to create simulations, create visualizations to better understand their data, and work in the field studying non-human primates. But all of us are interested at some level in understanding not only what it means to be human but how humans came to be. To learn this, we rely on the scientific meth-ods to study and evaluate theories about the past.

HOW CAN WE REALLY KNOW ABOUT THE PAST?

Contemporary bioanthropology relies on scientific inquiry and modern evolutionary theory to fully understand the processes of human evolution. But how can we actually learn anything about the remote past when there are no written records? We cannot access a time machine to test whether our ideas and theories are correct. This section examines how we can know what happened in the past and how we evaluate claims about human evolution.

How do we know a claim about the past (or a claim about any-thing for that matter) has any sort of validity from a scientific perspective. Bioanthropology revolves around creating and test-ing scientific hypotheses about human biology, human behavior, and human origins. Philosophers and historians of science have debated what makes a hypothesis scientific. There is no one definitive answer. But as a goal of this book is to understand where we come from, it is important to know how scientists compare different explanations of the past.

A scientific hypothesis is a statement about the world that is alleged to be true. But it must fit a few criteria. To use an example first used by the astrophysicist Carl Sagan, imagine I tell you that there is a fire-breathing dragon living in my garage. Is this a scientific hypothesis? In other words, can you test this claim? You are probably thinking, *yes, of course it is.* You can just go to my garage and look for yourself. So, I follow up by inviting you in to check out the garage. Maybe you see some boxes, a few tools, a few paint cans, but nothing else. Clearly there is no dragon there.

You might say to me 'I tested your dragon hypothesis and proved it wrong.' But I could come back and respond, 'Oh, I forgot to tell you: She is an invisible dragon!'

Could you test that hypothesis (e.g., I have an invisible fire-breathing dragon in my garage)? Maybe. You take some of the paint from the paint cans and throw the paint around the garage. Since the paint splatters to the ground you can say 'Hey, there is nothing here! I disproved it!' But then I rejoin with 'Oh I also forgot to tell you she has no mass … and before you try a heat sensor the dragon doesn't show up on the spectrum.'

The idea is that this becomes a pointless hypothesis to test. From a scientific perspective there is no difference between a not-showing-up-on-the spectrum, invisible, massless, fire breathing dragon and no dragon. The dragon *might* exist but since we cannot disprove its existence then there is no way to test it.

The dragon-in-my-garage example illustrates that a scientific hypothesis needs to meet three criteria: (1) it needs to be **reproducible**, meaning others can follow our steps and get the same results; (2) it needs to be **testable**, meaning that there is a way to assess it; and (3) it needs to be **falsifiable**, meaning that it can be proved wrong.

Falsifiability is important because it is difficult to prove something is true (it would be hard for me to prove to you the dragon is there given all my caveats). For that reason, scientists often set up hypotheses so that they can work to disprove them. In the above case, a better hypothesis would be that there is no dragon in my garage. That could be falsified easily by finding one dragon. We call such a claim the null hypothesis. Scientists will set up a null hypothesis and then try to disprove it. In doing so, they learn something about the world. In bioanthropology we might hypothesize that only *Homo sapiens* have chins. This is a good scientific hypothesis since it can be falsified by finding a fossil human ancestor that is older that our species that has a chin. Such a find would then prove that hypothesis wrong.

As we will see in Chapter 5, there have been several different explanations for why our ancestors began to walk on two legs. To evaluate different hypotheses we need a way to compare these different models. There is a quick shorthand known as **Occam's razor**, which says the simplest explanation is most likely to be the correct one. In this context 'simplest' means the theory that makes the least number of assumptions about the world.

Imagine someone tells you to pick a card from deck of playing cards. Then, without them looking at the card, they tell you which card you picked. One hypothesis is that they have ESP. Another valid hypothesis is that they cheated. ESP might exist but it is very controversial. The second hypothesis (i.e., that the person was using a magician's trick to learn the card without you knowing) assumes less about the world. It is a simpler hypothesis as it makes the least number of assumptions. Using Occam's razor, we should test that hypothesis first.

Scientists use hypothesis testing to build up facts about the world through research and studies. When we say something is a theory, we are saying that it is an explanation of a series of facts about the world, rather than suggesting it is not well supported. Theories might be wrong, and science aims to be self-correcting, but often times they are backed up by a lot of evidence. For instance, when thinking about change over time, we rely on the fact of evolution and the theory of natural selection. But at this point in time there is no reason at all to doubt that natural selection is an accurate model for explaining some evolutionary change.

While this book is not a theology text, it is always important to note that the scientific view of the past might conflict with religious views of where we come from. For readers interested in this topic, Steven Jay Gould's concept of non-overlapping magisteria is helpful. Gould argued that religion and science are different types of inquiry, with science documenting the natural world and religion searching for purpose and meaning. Most anthropologists are not dogmatic in their assertions about the past and can be religious.

It is also important to keep in mind that science is self-correcting. As we learn more about the world, we update our theories. 100 years ago, many anthropologists would say that humans are the only species to use tools, but we know now that tool use is much more widespread. As you learn more about bioanthropology and human evolution keep in mind how we test claims and build up evidence in support of various hypotheses.

The scientific study of the past is unique in many ways, since testing our models is not as easy as it might be in physics or chemistry. But over the last generations scholars have come up with ways to test our understanding of the past, as can be seen by the fact that bioanthropology is always being updating with new data and novel theories. With that in mind, the next step in thinking about bioanthropology is to learn what exactly was controversial about the ideas of evolution and natural selection in the first place. For that, we turn to the history of the study of the origins of species.

WHERE DID THE IDEA OF EVOLUTION BY NATURAL SELECTION COME FROM?

An oft-repeated story is that when Thomas Huxley (1825–1895) first learned about the idea of evolution by natural selection he replied, 'How extremely stupid not to have thought of that!' Many people have the same reaction. As detailed in this chapter, the basic idea of natural selection is that forces that act on the differences between individuals of the same species are similar to those that act on the differences between species. Usually, we are told that this idea was generated by Charles Darwin. But there is much more to this story.

This section provides an overview of why the idea of natural selection took so long to become accepted. It is also a short overview of the historical study of evolution by natural selection. Oftentimes, the discussion of how humans found out about their origins is very Eurocentric. It is important to remember that it is not true that science only advances through the work of these mostly white men. Rather people of color and women were often not allowed in the spaces where this type of research was undertaken.

Evolution is simply change over time. Many things can evolve, such as our opinions on a topic or our views on specific political issues. For biologists, evolution is about change in specific features of an organism's biology. We can ask large-scale questions that examine where species come from or look at the lower level, asking what changes happen between generations of the same species.

Biological evolution is predicated on the idea that species change over time. Aristotle (384–322 BCE) and other Greek philosophers taught that nature was hierarchical, with the gods at the top of this ladder. This 'Great Chain of Being' means that species are fixed in place in and cannot change. The reason for them being fixed (and not changing) is that each rung of the ladder needs to be filled with something. If one species were to change and become better or worse, it would move up or down the ladder. This would leave an open rung, something that the Greek philosophers thought could not happen since it went against their ideas of stability.

Because many scientists read and were influenced by the Greeks, they accepted this theory that species did not change. Some historians argue that it was this idea, the so-called 'fixity of the species,' that prevented ideas of evolution from being accepted. It took many generations before scholars in the Western tradition began to think about change over time.

What happened to bring about this change in the way philosophers and scientists thought about the world? Historian of science Janet Browne suggests the origins of evolutionary thought lies in the search for Noah's ark. Seventeenth-century scholars thinking about the diversity of plants and animals accepted the Bible as literally true. However, they had a problem. The Bible tells the story of the ark that Noah built to rescue the animals before the flood. After the flood, Noah let the animals off the ark to repopulate the Earth. If all animals had their origin point where Noah's ark landed (perhaps on Mount Ararat in Turkey), how did various animals get to be where they are today? They wanted to understand the reasons for the current distribution of species.

These scholars aimed to explain how animals arrived at their final destination. This research led to the study of the distribution of species in space and through time, known today as **biogeography**. Scholars begin to collect data on the location of different species. Quickly they notice a paradox: If all species are designed for their specific environment, how did they get there in the first place? If all life has a single origin point, how did diversification occur?

Taxonomy is the science of ordering things. But to do this, scholars needed a set way to discuss the animals and plants they were examining. To help with this issue, Swedish scholar Carl Linnaeus (1707–1778) wanted to have a way to think and write about the varied forms of life that were being studied. He created a system of classification known as **binomial nomenclature**, a version of which is still used today. While he was not the first to propose such a system, his version of this classification was the most popular one. This system refers to animals by two names: the first, known as the **genus**, and the second, known as the **species**. Technically, we use both when referring to an animal since a species name can be used for different genera. Humans, for example, are *Homo sapiens*. The genus name, *Homo*, tells us about the larger classification group it belongs to. The genus name is always capitalized and the species name is in lower-case. Species names are unique to specific genera, so that there is no confusion about what organism is being talked about.

Nowadays, the general taxonomic system has eight general levels, organized from most to least inclusive, as shown in Table 1.1. Technically, there are other ranks as well, such as *subphylum*, which is below phylum and above class. Importantly, when Linnaeus proposed this system these classifications were not seen to connote any sort of evolutionary relationship between species. Descent with modification was not part of their system of thought.

Science, it is important to remember, operates within the cultural and social norms of the day. Looking at Table 1.1, we can see that humans are put in the class Mammalia. While the characteristics that separate this class from others are numerous, Linnaeus picked mammary glands as the feature to base his naming on for a specific reason. He was against the practice of 'wet nursing,' wherein wealthy mothers had their children nursed by others (some estimates suggest 90% of wealthy Parisian children were being wet-nursed at the time). Linnaeus thought these practices violated the laws of nature and the nurses would pass on harmful traits to the babies. He used the word *mammal* to put emphasis on this relationship between mother and baby. We still use the word mammal today but few of us realize why that term came to be used.

Linnaeus argued that each animal was suited to its own environment and habitat. Reindeer are found in Northern Europe and their biology is well-suited to this cold climate. But there is a not so obvious problem with this concept: How did the reindeer get to these regions originally? If Noah's ark lands in Turkey how did the reindeer migrate north? Linnaeus and others were not thinking in terms of change over time. Because of this, they had difficulties with understanding biogeographic issues.

Politics and science interacted again with the work of Georges-Louis Leclerc (in later life called 'Comte de Buffon') (1707–1788). Besides being critical of Linnaeus, he had major complaints with the American colonies. Buffon had a vested interest in proving Europe was better that the Americas. As a naturalist, Buffon examined the animal world and argued that species degenerated, or declined, if they lived in poor environments or habitats. To prove this, he studied the differences between European and American species, arguing that animals in the Americas were weaker. The environment of the American continent was, Buffon claimed,

TABLE 1.1 An overview of the current taxonomic classification of contemporary humans.

Taxonomic ranks	Classification for human
Domain	Eukarya
Kingdom	Animalia
Phylum	Chordata
Class	Mammalia
Order	Primates
Family	Hominidae
Genus	*Homo*
Species	*sapiens*

hostile to the development of animals. He thought that while at its best nature is immobile, when the habitat is not good an animal will decline. Animals were worse in America, he claimed, due to the poor environment. In other words, he thought that species could transform over time. While not an evolutionist, Buffon's work (which was widely read and discussed) formed the basis of the ideas of descent with modification.

Another scholar who helped to set the stage for thinking about evolution is Thomas Malthus (1766–1834). Malthus was an economist who was deeply concerned with demography, population growth, and food production. He argued that humans respond to food abundances by having more children. This, he concluded, will eventually lead to more starvation, since population increases faster than the ability to produce food. Today, such a **Malthusian trap** is said to occur because the food supply grows at a linear rate while the population grows exponentially. While the validity of this idea is contested, Malthus's ideas were widely read and influenced many scholars thinking about ideas of overproduction.

In fact, Malthus's writings had a profound effect on Charles Darwin (1809–1882), one of the best-known scientists in history. Numerous biographies, documentaries, and movies have been created about him. During his five-year voyage on the HMS *Beagle*, Darwin worked on natural history collections and kept journals of his thoughts, making the voyage of the *Beagle* one of the most influential expeditions in the history of scientific thought. The usual story told is that after Darwin returned home, he took his research, collections, and notes and began to think about how species might change.

Darwin's key insight was that the types of differences seen *between* species (different beak types in birds, for example) are similar to those differences seen *within* a species. Those differences within a species, Darwin realized, can drive competition for limited resources.

We can summarize Darwin's observations and ideas about natural selection as follows:

1. Species over-reproduce within a generation, which means there are more individuals in a group than can survive. This idea most likely came from Darwin's reading of Malthus.

2. Every generation there is a struggle for existence due to competition over limited resources.
3. There is also variation among individuals of a species.
4. Some of these variations are more favorable in the current environment than other variants, giving those individuals with a favorable trait a better chance of survival because they can access those resources.
5. Animals with favorable traits will survive while those with unfavorable traits are less likely to survive. (This is sometimes called 'survival of the fittest,' although it is important to recognize that fitness is not always easy to define.)
6. Those organisms that survive tend to reproduce their specific variants by passing them on to their offspring. At the same time, those with unfavorable traits will have comparatively fewer offspring. Darwin did not, however, know the root cause of how these traits were passed on.
7. The accumulation of favorable hereditary traits can lead to the formation of a new species.

To give an example, imagine a population of butterflies. In this population there are differences in the coloration of their wings, with some having darker coloration and others having lighter coloration. If the environment is such that one color variant can better blend in with the trees, those individuals will have a greater likelihood of surviving since they won't be seen by predators. They are 'fitter' in a Darwinian sense than the other variants. Because of this, that version has a greater percentage of offspring who make up the next generation. Darwinian natural selection is about how these small changes over many, many years accumulate and lead to the formation of a new species.

Darwin, though, was not the only person to come up with this idea. Alfred Russel Wallace (1823–1913) is sometimes called the 'co-discoverer of natural selection.' He had similar ideas at almost the same time. Not being as wealthy or well-connected as Darwin, Wallace did fieldwork in the Amazon basin, collecting many samples of fauna. He hoped to bring these collections to Europe to cement his reputation as a scholar and give him access to researchers like Darwin. Sadly, when heading back home the ship he was on caught fire and he lost almost all his specimens he had spent the last four years collecting!

Tenacious, and in need of money, Wallace travelled to the Malay Archipelago in Southeast Asia to obtain more collections. While there he began to think about same questions Darwin and others had considered about species. He proposed what is known as the 'Sarawak Law' in 1858: *Every species has come into existence coincident both in space and time with a closely allied species.* His ideas were very similar to Darwin's, but at the time Darwin's hypotheses were not published (though he had been working on his book for many years) so Wallace had no way of knowing.

When he wanted to share his ideas with someone, Wallace sent it to Darwin, since he was one of the most famous and best networked people he knew of. Scholars debate the exact timing and response, but in the end both of their works were presented at a science society in 1858, with Darwin publishing *On the Origin of Species* in 1859, 20 years after he first started his research into the topic!

The story of evolution by natural selection as told above is centered on European scholars. There is evidence, however, of the concept of natural selection being older and appearing in the works of Islamic scholars. While historians of science have debated how similar their ideas really are, Al-Jahiz (776–868), an Islamic philosopher, wrote a volume about animals that has been suggested to indicate natural selection.

Even the general story of Charles Darwin as a lone genius leaves a lot out. Darwin's accomplishments would have been impossible without his knowledge of taxidermy, a skill he learned from a former slave named John Edmonstone. He also relied on the organizational talents of Syms Covington, a servant who was with Darwin on the *Beagle* and helped with his collections.

Scholars respond to the mood and cultural climate of a particular period of history, known as a zeitgeist. Darwin did not know about Al-Jahiz and other Islamic scholars who had similar ideas, just as he was not aware that at the same time he was writing these ideas, a Czech friar was thinking about how pea plants pass on their traits to their offspring. If he had it would be interesting to think about how he would put all this into context.

The idea of evolution by natural selection has been studied for over 150 years. It has never been proven wrong, though we have learned much more about how natural selection operates. We also know that there are other ways in which evolution can occur, which is the subject of the next chapter. Bioanthropology uses insights, research, and data gathered by evolutionary biologists, geneticists, and other biologists to better understand human evolution.

CLASSIFICATION TODAY

Bioanthropology, as practiced today, has its roots in the exploration of human variation that began well before Darwin published his work. In the 1700s, Enlightenment scholars in Europe read accounts of explorers meeting different kinds of people. These humans looked and behaved very differently than how they expected people to act. European scholars took as a starting point the idea that they could put humans into categories the same way as naturalists organized animals into groups (Linnaeus himself argued that there were different types or species of humans. In later editions of his book, Linnaeus put humans into 'subspecies' and then associated various behaviors with these groups, such as arguing that *Homo europaeus* were governed by laws).

Classification became the goal of early versions of anthropology. From this work the concept of race became formalized in Western thought. As will be talked about more in Chapter 3, how anthropologists think about and understand what race is (and what it is not) has significantly changed as we learned more about human biology.

As early anthropologists were trying to understand the different ways humans organize themselves into groups they connected their ideas of variation, biology, and rudimentary genetics to understand human variation, but often in insidious ways. Classifications such as savagery, barbarism, and civilization were applied to human cultural groups without much understanding of the people themselves.

Similarly, *The Doctrine of Discovery*, a fifteenth-century edict from the Catholic Church, gave explorers the right to claim areas inhabited by non-whites. This was used to justify slavery, as it would 'save' the souls of the indigenous peoples and spread the Catholic faith. It gave permission for Europeans to see their bodies and brains as superior to other people, and those who stole land were able to see themselves as 'discovering' that land. Colonialists in the United States applied these ideas to the Native populations of the American continent as well as to enslaved peoples, using their 'science' to justify ideas of inferiority.

Much of this rationalization occurred before the Darwinian revolution. It did not rely on ideas of natural selection, but later scholars began to apply Darwin's idea to social life, claiming that evolution proved that some populations of humans were more evolved away from the apes than others.

After Darwin, it became common to argue that that human societies evolved in the same way that species did. For many researchers it made sense to apply concepts of natural selection to different human populations. Lewis Henry Morgan (1818–1881) popularized the idea of social evolution. Based on his work with some Native American tribes, Morgan applied Darwin's ideas of change over time to social groups, arguing that human groups progress through three stages: savagery, barbarism, and civilization. For him and others, evolution was about progress. Morgan thought that all cultures would follow this three part system, similar to how humans have evolved to become the pinnacle of evolution. For scholars like Morgan studying different cultures, it seemed obvious that Europeans were the acme of evolution. People from 'civilized' areas would have bigger brains, they believed, than groups from less advanced societies.

The first biological anthropologists began to collect skulls from other populations and organized these crania into groups to prove their preconceived ideas that the European elites were at the pinnacle of evolutionary development.

All of this came to a head, so to speak, in the work of Samuel Morton (1799–1851), who studied the cranial capacity of different groups. He argued in his 1839 book *Crania Americana* that non-whites had smaller heads than whites, and Africans had smaller heads than Native Americans. Today, anthropologists differ on how Morton came to these conclusions, but later work has disproved his broad claims and assertions.

Anthropologists soon began pushing back on the assumptions that people from different parts of the world were inherently different at the biological level. Anthropologists like Edward Tylor (1832–1917) suggested that culture, not biology, explained the large difference between human groups. The different lifeways explorers were encountering were the result of different historical pathways, not different biologies. Today anthropologists have rejected ideas of **unilinear evolutionism**, which sees all societies as going through the same path, from savagery, to barbarism, to civilization. These racist models were the basis of much of the early anthropology and led nineteenth-century scientists to argue for the creation of 'human zoos,' where people of color were displayed for the enjoyment of a white audience.

Franz Boas (1858–1942), considered the 'father' of American anthropology, pushed back on these theories of unilinear evolutionism. Cultures, he and his students argued, might seem outwardly similar, but could be a result of diverse paths. To understand them, one must engage in anthropological research. He showed that racialized groups are the result not of biology but of culture, demonstrating that American-born children of immigrants had different skull shapes than their European-born parents. Boas's work demonstrated that the environment, more than genes, determined cranial form. From Boas onwards, anthropologists have understood categories such as gender and race are a product of culture, not biology.

In the 1950s scholars began to move away from a simple version of measuring skulls to a more holistic model. The field began to move from calling itself 'physical anthropology' and now is more commonly referred to as biological anthropology (or bioanthropology for short). This is to not only emphasize a break from the past but to also emphasize new models, ideas, and frameworks.

Today's bioanthropology is vastly different from its early roots as a racist endeavor. In one sense, the intellectual ancestors of our field are the ones who invented concepts like biological race. Today's practitioners are on the forefront of showing why that does not work. They study how the differential outcomes that exist between races occur not because there are 'racial' genes, but in social institutions and practices. Race, we now know, is a reality that is socially created and constructed.

CHAPTER SUMMARY

This chapter has centered on the questions of what anthropology is and how we came to know about biological evolution. Applying evolutionary frameworks to human biology allows us to better understand what creates and maintains variation. In the next chapter, we will see what the root causes of this variation are, and how genetics is opening up new avenues of exploration into how hominins became human.

1. Anthropology is about the study of human differences. Anthropologists want to understand the causes and consequences of human variation and use different methods and theories to accomplish this.
2. Scientific explanations of the past are often stated as a null hypothesis that other scholars try to disprove.
3. Charles Darwin's theory of natural selection states that the accumulation of favorable hereditary traits over many generations can lead to the formation of a new species.
4. The first scholars who studied human variation began with the assumption that human populations can be ranked and ordered. Later anthropologists showed how this assumption was faulty.

FURTHER READING

Browne, Janet. 1983. *The Secular Ark: Studies in the History of Biogeography.* Yale University Press. *Covers the history of biogeography and the lead up to the work of Charles Darwin.*

Charles, Mark and Soong-Chan Rah. 2019. *Unsettling Truths: The Ongoing, Dehumanizing Legacy of the Doctrine of Discovery.* IVP. *A discussion of the Doctrine of Discovery and its role in European colonialism.*

Fuentes, Agustín. 2015. Integrative Anthropology and the Human Niche: Toward a Contemporary Approach to Human Evolution. *American Anthropologist* 117(2): 302–315. https://doi.org/10.1111/aman.12248. *An overview of modern bioanthropology as an integrative discipline.*

Gould, Steven Jay. 1981. *The Mismeasure of Man.* W. W. Norton & Co. *While an older book, this covers the work of Samuel Morton and others. It critiques the ideas of intelligence tests that support racist notions of biological superiority.*

Gould, Stephen Jay. 1997. Nonoverlapping Magisteria. Natural History 106: 16–22. *Gould argues that science and religion are not necessarily in conflict but that they examine different realms of the experience of being human.*

Hà, Benjamin A., Kiana Foxx, Samantha T. Mensah, Paul H. Barber, and Rachel L. Kennison. 2023. Interdisciplinary Approaches to Advancing Anti-Racist Pedagogies in Ecology, Evolution, and Conservation Biology. *Trends in Ecology & Evolution* 38(8): 683–687. https://doi.org/10.1016/j .tree.2023.05.003. *This paper looks at how to incorporate anti-racism into class room pedagogy and discusses the roles of John Edmonstone and Syms Covington.*

Kaplan, Jonathan Michael, Massimo Pigliucci, and Joshua Alexander Banta. 2015. Gould on Morton, Redux: What Can the Debate Reveal about the Limits of Data? *Studies in History and Philosophy of Biological and Biomedical Sciences* 52: 22–31. *An overview of the debate about Morton's cranial data.*

King, Charles. 2020. *Gods of the Upper Air.* Doubleday. *An overview of the work of Boas and his students in using anthropology to understand differences.*

Raby, Peter. 2002. *Alfred Russel Wallace: A Life.* Princeton University Press. *The life and science of the co-discovered of natural selection.*

Sagan, Carl. 1995. *The Demon Haunted World.* Random House. *A good look at how to tell good science from pseudoscience.*

2

GENETICS

CHAPTER OVERVIEW

Chapter 1 discussed how scientists began to think about change over time. We learned that differences observed *between* species are similar to differences seen *within* a species. And that those differences within a species are at the heart of evolution by natural selection. But what is the root cause of these differences? And what other ways can species change over time apart from natural selection? In this chapter we look at the field of genetics, which is at the root of human variation. This chapter explores the ways in which genetic changes occur from one generation to the next, the main drivers of biological evolution.

Many people are aware that DNA is the source of our genetic code. But how exactly does DNA create the differences we see in the human species? After reading this chapter, you will understand how the genes we inherit from our ancestors intersect and interact with the environment to create variation in physical traits. We will also learn about the topic of heritability, an important concept in genetics. We then survey how we can use knowledge of genetics to model evolution at the small-scale (microevolution) and then apply these concepts to large-scale changes such as speciation (macroevolution).

WHAT IS INHERITANCE?

The reason why some people are tall and others are short, or why some people have black hair while others have blond hair, has to do with the interactions between internal mechanisms in our

DOI: 10.4324/9781003390442-3

bodies and the environment. Our physical traits and behaviors are influenced by both our genes and our environment but the extent to which they each play a role in the way we look and act is hotly debated. To understand this, we need to look at how genes work.

You may have read how the Czech Augustinian friar Gregor Mendel (1822–1884) discovered the 'laws of inheritance' while experimenting with pea plants. However, it is rarely made clear why he was doing this work in the first place. Why would a friar want to grow pea plants and record the shape of their seeds and the size of the plants over many generations?

Mendel and others like him were motivated partly by political and economic reasons. In the 1800s a major economic and political problem was how to make sure plants and animals that farmers raised would produce high quality grains and wool. But it was unclear how to do this. Countries wanted to be able to say their goods were the best, so money and time were invested in the question of what produces the best wool and other materials that the country could sell.

For example, it was believed that the environment was the key determining factor of the quality of wool a sheep could provide. Farmers had realized that if you tried to make local wool better by bringing in sheep with higher quality wool from another region, the desirable wool disappeared after a few generations. This degradation was attributed to the local environment. The working hypothesis was that the traits an animal brought with them disappeared quickly due to the climate being less conducive to good quality wool. This was a problem for regions that did not seem to have the correct climate!

Scholars such as Count Imre (Emmerich) Festetics (1764–1847) wanted to fully understand what was happening. He was a sheep breeder and the originator of the word 'genetics.' Festetics wanted to know why the fine, soft wool of Merino sheep disappeared after a generation or two when brought to places like the Czech Republic. He realized that by inbreeding his sheep he could concentrate the good traits in specific lines. After observing the results, Festetics proposed 'laws' of inheritance. He noticed that healthy animals can pass on their specific characteristics. He also noted that traits of grandparents may reappear in later generations. Finally, he observed that animals with desirable traits that have been inherited over many generations can sometimes have offspring with traits that are different.

Festetics's work did not receive a lot of attention at the time, but his ideas echo what later studies found: An organism's characteristics are the result of the environment they develop in along with traits they inherit from their parents. And as with Charles Darwin's work, his story reminds us that the idea of a 'lone genius' is problematic. Scientists work within research networks and the norms of a society. Gregor Mendel is justly famous, but he too was part of this larger quest to find ways to make better quality crops and animals.

The section that follows is a brief overview of what scientists have learned about the process of inheritance, the transmission from parent to offspring of genetic material. To learn this, scholars needed to first understand what exactly is being passed down from one generation to the next.

BIOLOGY OVERVIEW

Genetic material is housed in the **cell**, the basic unit of life. Cells contain the molecules that an organism relies on to perform needed functions and tasks. For our purposes, some of the most important parts of the cell are the nucleus, which is the source of most of the genetic material, and the **mitochondria**. The mitochondria produce a cell's energy and also are the source of a specific type of DNA called mitochondrial DNA, or mtDNA.

Inside the nucleus of many cells is where the nuclear DNA is stored in strands known as **chromosomes**. If you were to lump all the chromosomes together and record the molecular information stored therein you would have the **genome** of an organism. A person's **phenotype** is their observable characteristics. Phenotype is controlled by two primary factors: their genetic code, called a **genotype**, and their environment.

Many human cells have 23 pairs of chromosomes: 22 pairs of autosomes and one pair of sex chromosomes. In humans, we refer to the sex chromosomes by their general shape, X and Y. We are often told that females have two X chromosomes (XX) and males have one X and one Y (XY), but as we will see in Chapter 3 nature is much more complex than this.

The fact that human chromosomes come in pairs tells us something very important. In species that reproduce sexually, one member of each homologous pair of chromosomes is inherited from each biological parent, coming from their sex cells (sperm and egg). Species that reproduce sexually have one set of DNA from their mom and one from their dad. Cells that have both sets of chromosomes are called diploids. Most human cells are diploids, having two sets of chromosomes, but this differs in other species. Polyploidy is often seen in plants. Potatoes have four sets of chromosomes, while strawberries have eight. Geneticists can make use of polyploidy in interesting ways: Seedless watermelons, for instance, are intentionally made with three chromosomes to prevent them from making seeds.

The sex cells, or gametes, are different in that they only have *one* set of chromosomes rather than the usual homologous pairs, called the haploid number. Most species that reproduce sexually have two types of gametes: a larger version called the ova (or egg) and a smaller version called the sperm. The reason why sex cells only have one set of chromosomes is because the egg cell needs to fuse with a sperm cell for reproduction to occur, with sexual reproduction being the union of the two types of gametes. In sexual reproduction the offspring has a 'mix' of both parents, with offspring have only about 50% of one parent's genetic material.

In asexual reproduction, there is no chromosome reduction or fertilization. Asexual reproduction makes an almost exact copy. Your offspring is your clone. Your genes spread and you do not need to worry about competing for and finding a mate. An organism that reproduces asexually does not need to attract a mate, which limits the competition between different members of the same species.

Sexual reproduction, however, leads to more variation. In sexual reproduction a sperm and an ovum combine to form a zygote which has a new combination of genetic material. As we will learn throughout this book, variation is good for an organism. But relying on this type of reproduction means looking for a mate, which is not always easy. Searching for a partner is the source of much of the variation we see in a species. One of the most famous examples of this is a male peacock's feathers, which he uses to show off and attract a mate.

The sex cells are created via a process known as meiosis. It begins with a parent cell that is diploid and during the cellular division an individual cell 'loses' half its chromosomes. The parent cell undergoes two cycles of cell division, leaving off with four new cells, each with the haploid number of chromosomes. While a body cell has 46 chromosomes, a sex cell has only 23 chromosomes.

The genome stored in an individual's genetic code is one of the main sources of variation. The basis of this variation has to do with the structure of DNA. In DNA there are four bases called nucleotides: adenine [A], guanine [G], thymine [T], and cytosine [C]. Adenine always bonds with thymine and guanine always bonds with cytosine. They connect to each other in a twisted ladder-shaped molecule that is called a double helix. This helix shape gives DNA two powerful properties: It can both duplicate itself and store information. The exact way DNA can do these two things is very complex and not that relevant for us. Rather, a quick summary is all we need to answer the question of what a biological parent passes on to its offspring.

The processes by which a cell 'reads' the DNA and then follows the instructions is known as transcription and translation. Briefly, every 3 bases in the DNA molecule is a signal to the cell. This group of 3 bases, called a codon, codes for a specific amino acid. Another molecule known as RNA reads the codons in order, chaining amino acids together into one molecule. The chain continues until the RNA gets to a special sequence of three bases called the 'stop codon' that signals the cell to stop adding to the chain. In sum, DNA is a note to the cell to chain together different amino acids. These chains of amino acids are called proteins.

An important aspect of the system of the genetic code is that it is redundant. This means that many of the amino acids are coded by more than one codon. The amino acid lysine's DNA codon is AAG and AAA. This redundance means that is there is a mutation in the DNA and one of the bases gets mutated or changed into another base, it is possible that while the DNA itself is different the gene is expressed in the same way. This allows for some tolerance of mutations.

The second characteristic of DNA is that it can duplicate itself. This is due to its double helix shape and is a complex biochemical

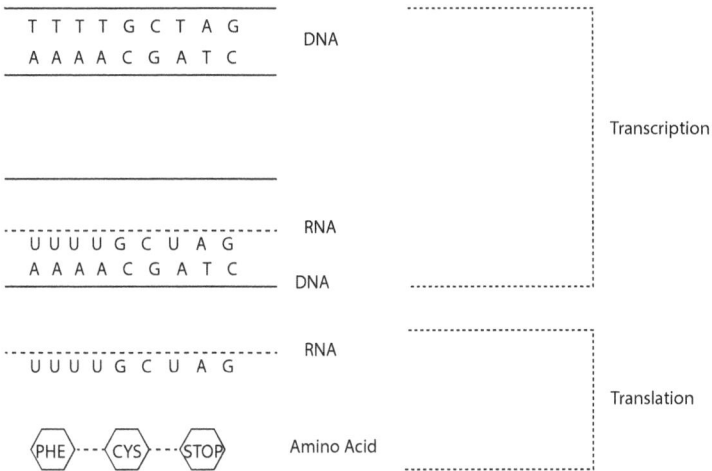

Figure 2.1 Simplified overview of transcription and translation. During transcription the two strands of DNA open up and the RNA reads one of the strands. Then, during translation, RNA codons build up amino acid chains. Here, the final codon is a 'stop,' telling the cell to cease adding amino acids to the chain.

process. When the molecule is making copies, there are sometimes glitches, or mutations, in the genetic bases. This means that a thymine might be altered to a cytosine. These mutations can occur randomly and can be the result of exposure to certain types of radiation.

GENETICS

A region of DNA that codes for a protein or that regulates the production of a protein is called a **gene**. Genes can also be thought of as units of the genome that have functional information in them. Different versions of the same gene are known as **alleles**. Since humans have two copies of each gene, one from their mom and one from their dad, they inherit two alleles for each gene on an autosome (the non-sex chromosomes).

In a simple Mendelian inheritance system, a **dominant** allele is one that masks the presence of the other trait, while a **recessive** one is the masked trait. Imagine in a flowering plant there is a gene for flower color and two alleles: one for yellow petals and one for red petals. Assuming this pea plant is a diploid it has two copies of each gene. If it inherits the same allele from both its parents it is said to be **homozygous** at that region, or **locus**. If it inherits different alleles then it is **heterozygous**. **Heterozygosity** is often used as a measure how much variation there is in a population.

In the example of pea plants, if the red petal allele is dominant, that would mean that if the pea plant were heterozygous for that gene the plant's *genotype* would be one red allele and one yellow allele and the plant's *phenotype* would be to have red petals. Genotypes are often represented by the first letter of the dominant trait, so in this case the heterozygote condition can be written as (Rr).

The more heterozygous an organism, group, or species is, the more variation there is in that population's background. Likewise, an organism that is very homozygous is one that has inherited many of the same allele pairs. A homozygous individual is likely coming from a population that has had a lot of inbreeding in the past.

If you are curious how this works at the molecular level, in a basic dominant/recessive system the dominant allele gives the cell instructions to make a protein. The recessive allele has a slightly different code, perhaps swapping out one amino acid for another due to a mutation in the DNA that led to a different codon being read. This can create a different phenotype as it changes the molecular makeup of the protein.

When Mendel did his work on pea plants, one of the traits he studied was round and wrinkled seeds. He noted that wrinkled seeds are recessive and the smooth seeds are dominant. We now know that wrinkled seeds occur when a plant does not inherit a

TABLE 2.1 How genotype relates to phenotype in a simple Mendelian inheritance system.

Genotype	Phenotype	Allele pair type
RR	Red	Homozygous dominant
Rr	Red	Heterozygous
rr	Yellow	Homozygous recessive

copy of a starch-binding enzyme. Without this enzyme, the plant has a higher sugar content (since the sugar is not being converted to starch). This means it takes in more water and eventually leads to the wrinkled appearance as it dries out.

We say a trait is Mendelian when it is affected by one gene that has dominant and recessive alleles. For most human traits the situation is much more complex, with most traits being influenced by multiple genes. For example, you may have read that tongue rolling is Mendelian. This, though, is not the case. Other examples that are not controlled by one gene are shown in Table 2.2. Much of the data in this table comes from John H. McDonald's excellent website on myths of human genetics (https://udel.edu/~mcdonald/mythintro.html).

In general, few traits that we notice in humans are totally Mendelian. For the most part the traits we observe are controlled by more than one gene; in other words they are polygenetic. Such traits are caused by the interaction of multiple genes and the environment.

HERITABILITY

The past few pages have been full of complex biology. It took generations of scholars to figure out these processes and there is still much to uncover. The key lesson is that the information in the DNA is expressed within an environmental context. DNA

TABLE 2.2 Non-Mendelian human traits.

Trait	Myth	Reality
Phenylthiocarbamide tasting	Ability to taste PTC is controlled by one allele	There are other genes and environmental factors that influence this
Eye color	Blue eyes recessive to alleles for non-blue eyes	More complex and determined by numerous gene interactions
Hitchhiker's thumbs	Some people can bend top of thumb backwards but this is a recessive trait	Thumb bending is a continuous trait and not discrete

is packaged in chromosomes, which come in pairs, with most humans have 23 pairs of chromosomes. Genes are instructions that tell the cell what to do (e.g. a gene for ear wax type), while alleles are different versions of a gene.

Imagine there is an allele that produces a hormone that has been shown to add 5 millimeters (approximately 0.2 inches) to a person's height. We might think that means that anyone who has that allele will be taller than someone without it. But other alleles might impact that gene's effect. And, more importantly, the environment can play a role here too. A person could have multiple alleles throughout her genome that gives her the likelihood of being very tall, but that only would occur if she has access to good nutrition.

This leads us to a very important concept known as **heritability**, which is the amount of phenotypic variation that can be explained by genotypic variation within a specific population and environment. Imagine you are at a track meet and examine the players on the field. Some will be taller than others. Heritability tells us how much of that variation is because they have different genes. But in this case, we have the problem that we do not know if all the athletes had the same environment. To measure heritability we need to study organisms that have the same environment. And in humans that is very hard to do. To solve this problem, behavioral geneticists will often study identical twins reared apart, with the assumption that they have the same genetics but different environments. Or, they look for families that have both identical and fraternal twins. These twin studies have proven very interesting but are not without their critics who point out that the assumptions of the environmental differences or similarities might be incorrect.

While colloquially we might use the terms heritability and inheritance to mean the same thing, there is actually an important difference. The heritability of number of fingers in humans is very low, since most of the variation we see in the number of fingers is due to non-genetic factors such as accidents. But the number of fingers on one hand is inherited, since it is a primitive trait that comes from our primate ancestry. Inheritance looks at how a gene influence the average levels of a trait while heritability measures how a gene influences variation among people in levels of that trait.

With all this in mind, I find it helpful to think of DNA not as a blueprint but rather as a cookbook. A professional cook following a complicated recipe would probably have a perfect meal in the end. Now imagine a novice cook is following the same recipe. Would they have the same results? Probably not. Maybe there were implicit steps that the amateur cook did not know about. Or maybe the professional cook's kitchen has a high-end oven that keeps better temperature. Or the novice lives at a high altitude and did not adjust the recipe. Or maybe they skipped an important step without noticing it (for example, they could have forgotten to put the food in the oven). The whole developmental system that produces an organism is the attempt to cook that dinner. You might start with the same system but end up very different due to the environmental system.

EVOLUTIONARY THEORY

Imagine you come across a new species. It looks kind of like a dog but has long legs and a short tail. As a trained biological anthropologist one of the first questions you might ask is why did this species evolve such long legs? It is relatively easy to come up with some hypotheses to explain this (longer legs allows the dog to walk further, lets the dog remove heat quicker, etc.). However, it also could be that the trait has no adaptive value whatsoever. In the next section we will talk about the different ways traits can evolve, linking Darwin's work from the previous chapter with that of genetic theory.

Population genetics examines genetic variation within and between populations. It was developed in the early part of the twentieth century as a bridge between Darwinian evolution and Mendelian inheritance. At the time, there was debate between scholars that studied inheritance (representing the Mendelian school of genetics that thought evolution occurred through large mutations) and those that studied evolution (these scholars followed Darwinian natural selection and focused on small changes over the long term). Population genetics uses mathematical models to predict the ways in which the number of alleles in a population can change over generations.

From the perspective of genetics, **biological evolution** is a change in allele frequency from one generation to another. In other words, evolution happens when these is a change in the percentage of alleles over time in a population. Because it revolves around frequencies, biological evolution applies only to populations rather than to an individual. This is because a person's genotype is set at birth. Evolution requires there to be genetic variation. If every organism is the same, then nothing can change at the genetic level unless a new variant emerges.

This fact is the basis of one of the most fundamental principles in population genetics, Hardy–Weinberg equilibrium: $p^2 + 2pq + q^2 = 1$.

In this equation, p is the frequency of the dominant allele and q is the frequency of the recessive allele. While the equation might seem daunting, at one level it just reminds us that when we add up the frequencies of the alleles for a gene, that number should equal one.

But, genetic variation only remains constant in the absence of outside factors. The equation is saying is that in the absence of outside forces, the genetic variation within a population does not change from one generation to the next.

Hardy–Weinberg equilibrium is the null hypothesis of evolution, telling us what to expect to find when evolution is not occurring. As the null hypothesis we often expect to reject it and then ask why the population does not fit the predicted model. In other words, populations not in Hardy–Weinberg equilibrium are being affected by factors that change the allele frequencies. We call these factors that affect the frequency of alleles over subsequent generations the forces of evolution and they are the main driving factors in evolution. While there is some debate about how many exist some of the most important ones are recombination, mutation, gene flow, random genetic drift, and natural selection.

THE FORCES OF EVOLUTION

Recombination is the exchange of DNA between the paternal and maternal chromosomes. Recall that genes are found on specific chromosomes. Since we inherit these chromosomes from our parents, it would make sense that genes are inherited as a cluster. For example, maybe in a rodent population there is a gene for eye color on the same chromosome where there is a gene for fur color.

A parent who passes on their eye color allele to their child would also pass on their hair color allele since the genes are linked on the chromosome. That means that if she has an allele for white fur and an allele for yellow eyes they would be inherited together since they are on the same chromosome.

But that is not always what happens. During meiosis the pairs of chromosomes sometimes exchange genetic material. This process is known as recombination. If not for recombination specific alleles on a chromosome would always be grouped together as they get passed down from parent to offspring. Recombination lets alleles move between homologous chromosomes (they don't do this with intent. Recombination is mostly a random process).

As discussed in Chapter 3, sex differentiation is partly based on a gene (the SRY gene) on the Y chromosome that tells a cell to make specific hormones. Due to their size and shape differences, X and Y chromosomes rarely crossover, but sometimes they do. If the part of the Y that has the SRY allele crosses over to the X chromosome, then the person who inherits that X could develop along the male typical path even though they do not have a Y chromosome in their genotype. This is rare, happening in 1 in 20,000 cases.

This 'scrambling' of linked genes gives natural selection more variation to work with. It creates variation within and among chromosomes. It does not result in new alleles but does shift the ways in which existing alleles are combined.

A **mutation** is a direct change to the DNA sequence. This can happen for many reasons and is the only way to for a new allele to appear in a closed gene pool that has no migrants moving into it. Point mutations, where a single nucleotide is substituted for another nucleotide, occur often. The number of novel mutations in each human seems to range between 30-80. Since the genetic code is redundant, some of these mutations are silent, meaning they do not cause any change in a person's phenotype. Other mutations create functional changes during protein synthesis. Whether most mutations are bad or neutral is unclear, but if a mutation is beneficial there is a chance it will get passed onto the next generation.

Random mutations can have significant impacts on human history. My favorite example of this comes from the time leading up

Time 1   Time 2

Group A

Group B

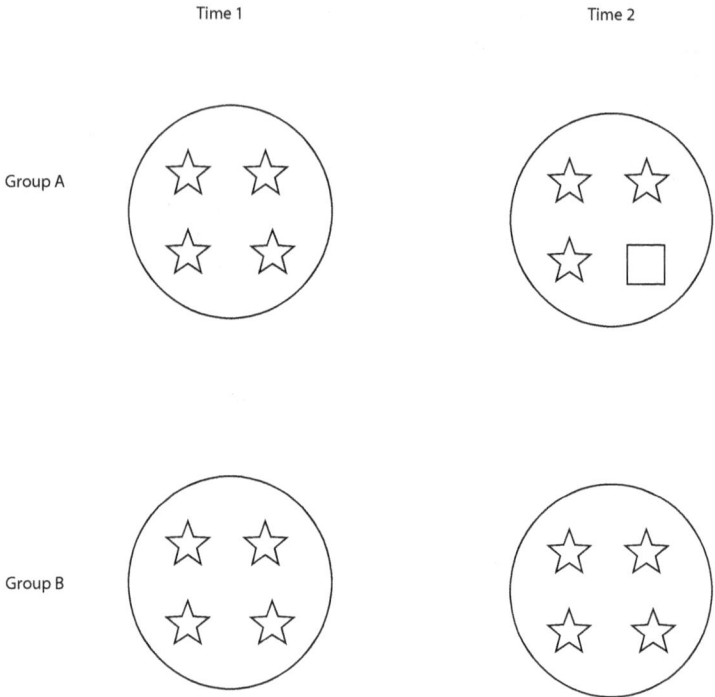

Figure 2.2 Image showing how a mutation changes the allele frequencies. At time 1, both groups have the same types of alleles. But a mutation at time 2 has increased the differences within group 1 and between group 1 and group 2.

to the Russian Revolution. Grigori Rasputin (1869–1916) was a Russian monk who gained a lot of power because he could apparently heal Alexei Nikolaevich (heir to the Russian throne). Alexi suffered from hemophilia, a blood clotting disorder he inherited from his maternal great-grandmother Queen Victoria. She had a random mutation in her X chromosome that made her a carrier for a recessive hemophilia trait. As most women have two X chromosomes, they are often **carriers** of this condition but do not express it since the allele on their other X chromosome is functional.

Alexei inherited her recessive hemophilia allele and, as a male, did not have a second X chromosome to counteract its affects. Rasputin was somehow able to heal Alexei when he was injured and stop him from bleeding. This gave Rasputin a lot of power, power that many other Russians did not appreciate due to his controversial reputation. Some have suggested that his power over the royal family helped to lead to the overthrow of the Tsarist family.

Importantly, mutations can only spread out of the gene pool if an organism migrates. **Gene flow** is the movement of an allele from one population to another. When a member of a group migrates to a new population, and then interbreeds, they add their genetic material to the next generation's gene pool. This affects the allele frequencies of the subsequent generation. In humans, these gene flow events are fairly common as we are a globalized species. One example of extreme gene flow is the case of Genghis Khan's (1162– 1227) Y-chromosome. As the founder of the Mongol Empire, he spread his genes wide. Some work has suggested that 16 million men worldwide share his Y-chromosome. Other founders had similar large effects, such as Niall Noígíallach (Niall of the Nine Hostages), a king of Ireland who died around 405 CE.

Importantly, as we will see in Chapter 3, gene flow has kept human populations from becoming very different. One way we look at this is through F_{st}, which expresses the proportion of total group variation that can be accounted for by between-population differences. F_{st} ranges from 0, in which case all the variation is found within a group and there are no genetic differences between groups, to 1 where the diversity is partitioned out among populations and there are no genetic differences within a group. If F_{st} is 1, all of the differences are between groups. In other words, the closer F_{st} is to 1 the greater effect these subgroups have on diversity. F_{st} decreases rapidly as gene flow increases. See the next chapter for how F_{st} is used.

Natural selection, as discussed in Chapter 1, is the mechanism through which an organism best suited to the environment survives and passes on its genes. Genotypes are replicated at different rates due to a difference in how those genotypes interact with the environment. Natural selection occurs when there is differential reproductive success, with fitness being a measure of the number of gametes a phenotype passes on to the next generation. In this sense, natural selection is the evolutionary force most responsible for adaptation to the environment.

Sexual selection is sometimes seen as a part of natural selection and other times seen as a distinct evolutionary force. It acts on an organism's ability to obtain a mate. A species with high reproductive variance (i.e., where some individuals have many offspring and others have few or none), will often have stronger effects of sexual selection. Its role in humans is hotly debated, but as we shall see some think that mating practices had a large effect on human evolutionary history. Sexual selection can produce characteristics that are harmful to an individual's ability to survive but that signal to a potential mate that they are strong enough to survive. For example, colorful plumage and songs is a costly signal in some birds, showing off to mates and predators alike where they are located.

The last force of evolution is one of the more difficult to understand, **genetic drift**. Drift refers to random changes in allele frequencies from one generation to the next and is the result of sampling biases in allele frequencies. There are a finite number of gametes to sample from in each generation and random events occur that bias which alleles are represented in the next generation.

This is probably the most difficult force to conceptualize. Imagine you place five red and five blue marbles into a vase. Those marbles represent two different alleles, both of which make up 50% of the total population for the first generation. You now take a marble at random, note its color, and put it back into the vase. Do this ten times to represent the next generation of alleles. In mathematical terms you sample from the vase with replacement. This time around, you happened to end up with seven red and only three blue marbles:

- **First generation**: *red, red, red, red, red, blue, blue, blue, blue, blue*
- **Second generation**: *red, red, red, red, red, red, red, blue, blue, blue*

In the second generation the allele frequencies have changed, with 70% of the marbles being red and only 30% being blue. But this change is not due to a mutation, gene flow, or natural selection but rather just to the randomness and chance inherent in sampling from a population. That randomness is the basis of genetic drift.

In the natural worlds, genetic drift is seen when floods or other random events occur. The individuals who survive these events can pass their alleles to the next generation while those who died before they reproduced cannot. But note that survival here has nothing to do with fitness.

Figure 2.3 shows the results of a computer program that simulates genetic drift. These fluctuations are not correlated with reproductive success but caused by chance differences in reproduction. Genetic drift is correlated with sample size. It is more powerful in small populations as random events are more powerful when there are less individuals. In Figure 2.3, drift has a larger effect when the population size is set to 20 then when it was set to 2000. However, in the absence of other forces, genetic drift will eventually lead to one allele being at 100% and the other alleles going extinct. In this case, an allele that is shared with everyone in the population is said to be 'fixed.'

Examples of genetic drift include **population bottlenecks**, events where a large percentage of the population is prevented from reproducing due to a volcanic eruption or other natural disaster. In 1775 a typhoon hit the island of Pingelap in Micronesia. This sadly devastating event caused a population bottleneck among the island residents. One of the few survivors was completely colorblind. As that person's descendants has children, the trait spread in the subsequent population, with around 10% of the island's population today being colorblind due to the effects of genetic drift on the small population that survived the typhoon. Since being colorblind did not seem to be causally linked to surviving the tropical storm, the spread of this allele is an example of how genetic drift works. This **founder's effect**, when allele frequencies in a small group of founders may be different (by chance) from their original population, is also an example of genetic drift.

Inbreeding is extreme genetic drift. The end of the Spanish Hapsburg dynasty, which lasted from 1516–1700, shows how cultural behaviors shape evolution. This family often married within their lineage. Around 80% of the marriages were between people descended from the same recent ancestor, what anthropologists call consanguineous. To be clear, consanguineous marriage is far from uncommon and most of the time does not lead to significant

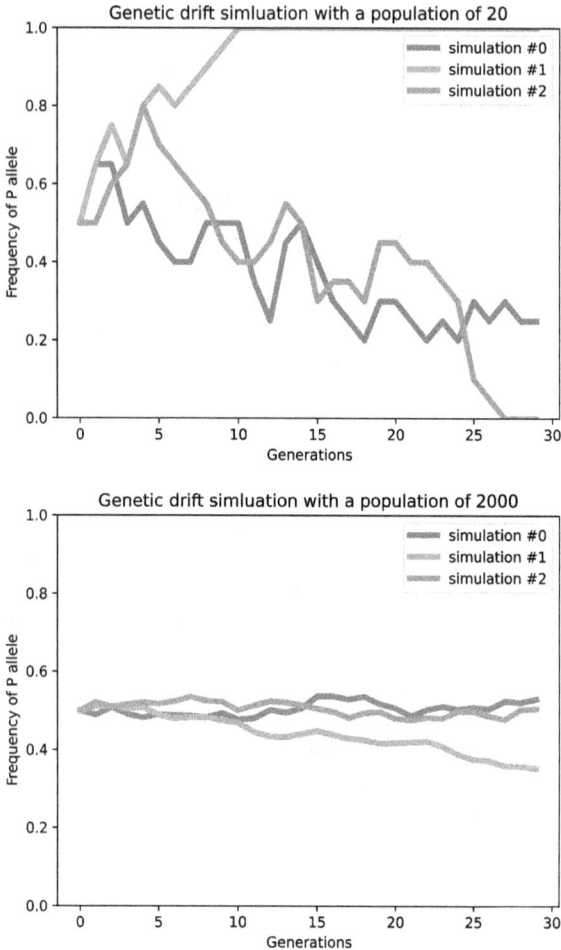

Figure 2.3 Results of a computer program that simulates genetic drift. On the x-axis is time, measured in generations. On the y-axis is the frequency of one allele. This model assumes that mutation, gene flow, and natural selection are not occurring. In the first simulation, there are only 20 people in the population. Due to the small population, in the first run the random effects of drift removes the allele while in the third run it fixes the allele at 100% of the population. But the second graph shows what happens when the population is larger. Here, drift does not have enough time to remove the variation.

problems. But the Habsburgs intermarried so often to preserve their royal bloodline that it had deleterious effects on their bloodline. The inbreeding coefficient of some of its members was 0.2, which means that 20% of that person's genes are identical because the alleles come from the same ancestor! This extreme inbreeding may have been why the last Spanish Hapsburg King, Charles II was unable to have children. Charles II's inbreeding coefficient suggests that he carried identical copies for more than one-fourth of his genes.

Table 2.3 gives an short overview of the various forces discussed and their overall effect on a population. All these forces play a role in evolution. Natural selection is adaptive, which means it is a function of the fitness properties of individuals. It also requires there to be variation. Natural selection acts over time to destroy the variation which it feeds upon. Drift, mutation, and recombination are sometimes referred to as the nonadaptive forces of evolution as they are not affected by forces operating on a phenotype. Being nonadaptive does not mean they are not important. Random genetic drift, for example, can 'fix' deleterious alleles due to its stochastic nature. They all influence how an organism can respond to pressure, something we will look at more in Chapter 3.

Understanding how these forces work allow geneticists to link the microevolutionary changes at the level of genes to the macroevolutionary changes that produce new species. Sometimes called the **modern synthesis**, this work combines the science covered in the last two chapters to create mathematical models of

TABLE 2.3 Overview of the forces of evolution.

Force	Effects
Recombination	Increases diversity by creating new combinations
Mutation	increase diversity within & between populations
Gene Flow	increases diversity within a population and decreases diversity between populations
Natural Selection	Can decreases diversity within a population by selecting for one phenotype
Genetic drift	Reduces variation within a population over time

evolution. The modern synthesis sees the gene as the unit that natural selection acts upon. It demonstrated that evolution is gradual and caused by small genetic changes.

In the last few decades some scholars have suggested the need for an **extended evolutionary synthesis**, which argues constructive development (organisms shape their own development) and reciprocal causation (developing organisms are not just the products, but also the cause of, evolution) should be incorporated into this framework. Scholars who support this framework often see niche construction as an important driver in evolution. This has been the source of much debate between vocal members of both camps.

Population geneticists rely on complex mathematical models and statistical methods to understand the allele frequencies of different populations, both extinct and extant. A related field is quantitative genetics, which studies traits that vary continuously, like height, that are the result of the interaction of multiple genes. Due to the complexities of this work, quantitative genetics often measures phenotypic traits and uses those measurements as correlates for genetic data. This type of work has allowed anthropologists studying human evolution to ask questions such as which evolutionary forces produced the differences we see between contemporary and past humans.

WHERE DO NEW SPECIES COME FROM?

Mathematical equations from population and quantitative genetics have allowed researchers to model complex trait evolution over subsequent generations. But the connections between these small-scale changes and the differences between species are important. If these changes are the source of variation, how does this variation lead to new species? **Speciation** is the process of the formation of a new species.

Part of the problem here is that there is no single definition of species. Is the red wolf (a small wolf that is found in southeastern parts of the United States) an admixture of the wolf and the coyote, a subspecies of the gray wolf, or a third, distinct species? These questions can affect the legal protective status of populations, so it is far from simply an academic question.

It turns out that it is not easy to define a species. The most famous species definition is the **biological species concept**. This definition says that a species is a population of interbreeding organisms, reproductively isolated from all other populations in nature. It is difficult to apply this to fossil species since we cannot observed their reproduction. Moreover, many species seem to not follow these rules: tigons (male tiger and female lion), ligers (male lion and female tiger), zebroids (zebra-equine mix), grolar bears (grizzly-polar bear), and other hybrids have made scientist realize that species boundaries are more fluid.

The **phylogenetic species concept** argues that a species is defined by at least one unique, derived feature. It emphasizes shared decent and morphological differences between groups. Meanwhile, the **evolutionary species concept** sees a species as a genetic lineage of organisms with a beginning, a shared evolutionary trajectory, and a shared evolutionary fate. This too has its issues, since it can be hard to recognize species in the fossil record.

Most speciation events occur when two populations of the same species are separated by a barrier that prevents gene flow. The two populations become distinct and accrue different alleles and different behavioral repertoires. When that barrier is lifted the two groups may be different enough that they no longer recognize each other as potential mates. The two populations are now two different species. This is what happened with the Galápagos finches. They formed numerous species due to being isolated from one another on different islands.

Speciation can occur without barriers as well, and has been seen to occur in cichlid fish perhaps due to sexual selection.

The obvious question here, and one relevant for human evolution, is how long it takes for speciation to occur. In other words, when does one species become two? This is not easy to answer. Some cichlid fish seem to have speciated in 12,000 years. For mammals it seems to take more close to 2 million years.

INVESTIGATING ADAPTATION

Go back to the example above where you stumble upon a new species that resembles a dog with long legs. We now know a lot more about what sorts of questions we can ask about its traits. Why, for example, does it have such a short tail?

For any trait we examine from an evolutionary perspective, we need to ask a few salient questions. First off, is it independent of other traits? In other words, does it exist as a response to selection on a different part of the body? Perhaps it has a short tail because the gene that regulates tail length also regulates something else novel about the organism. It is often hard for evolutionary biologists and biological anthropologists to discern what features were selected and which exist because of other reasons.

While discussed in more depth in the next chapter, an adaptation is a trait or characteristic that allows an organism to survive and to reproduce in an environment for which it might not be able to survive without that trait. Adaptations give biologists clues as to the kinds of pressures a species faces to survive. For instance, if you compare pupil shape (the part of the eye that lets in light) in various mammals you would notice that some have vertical slits and others have horizontal slits. Ambush hunters, such as cats, have evolved vertical pupil shape so they can better judge the distance of prey, while prey animal like sheep have wider pupils that give them better panoramic vision.

An adaptation is something that gives an organism a selective advantage. In humans we think traits like walking on two legs and having larger brains were products of natural selection. Other aspects of human phenotype could also count. Tina Lasisi and colleagues looked at human scalp hair and argued that it plays an adaptive role in thermoregulation, reducing solar radiation to the scalp. Moreover, tightly curled hair provides even more protection. But we need to remember that not all traits are adaptive.

It is difficult, however, to demonstrate why a specific trait exists and if it is an adaptation or not. As we learned above, genetic drift can also affect the frequency of a trait. If a species underwent a population bottleneck 200,000 years ago and, as the population rebounded, the individuals with brown eyes became more common due to drift, that could lead to a species of mostly brown-eyed individuals. A biologist studying that population today might not realize why brown-eyed organisms predominate and could come up with an explanation based on fitness that was incorrect.

A common morphological trait may have evolved for a specific reason, or it could be the result of random genetic drift, a force of evolution that seems to have played a major role in human evolution. Some anthropologists think that specific characteristics of the human face are the result of drift rather than natural selection. Because of this scientist are careful to weight the effects of drift and selection and have developed theoretical frameworks to study these differences.

Moreover, features could exist for reasons that have nothing to do with its current use. A **spandrel** is a feature that is the byproduct of the evolution of some other characteristic. For example, we might ask if the presence of a chin in contemporary humans was adapted or is simply a byproduct of other mechanisms. Some scholars have suggested that language is a spandrel. In this view, our ability to use language is the byproduct of us having large brains.

Other times, species co-opt a trait for something that was not its intended purpose. For example, some egrets will use their wings to cast a shadow on the water, making it easier for them to spot fish. Such **exaptations** may be more common than we think.

Another key issue in evolutionary anthropology is understanding the relationships between species, both those that are still living and extinct species known only from the fossil record. By examining an organism's characteristics, biologists create 'trees' that show the evolutionary relationship between different species (Figure 2.4).

Taxonomy is classification based on shared characteristics. Taxonomic groups do not necessarily reflect evolutionary relatedness. The group of animals that fly, for example, consist of many different species that do not share a close common ancestor.

Creating these evolutionary trees requires understanding the relationships between species and being able to classify species on the basis of traits that link them together. Amphibians, for example, are all cold-blooded and have vertebrae (backbones). **Phylogeny** is the study of the relatedness, in evolutionary terms, of organisms. Phylogenies are created by looking for shared, derived traits that link different species together into **clades**, sets of species that include a common ancestor and all of its descendants. Primates are a clade since they include the first primate and every species that descended from that.

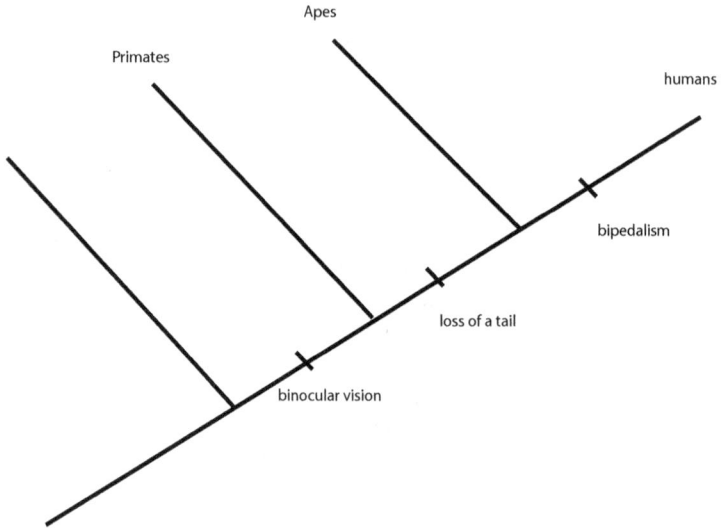

Figure 2.4 A basic cladogram.

While creating clades we distinguish between **primitive** traits that are present in the common ancestor (such as live birth in dogs and wolves due to the fact that they are mammals) and **derived** traits that are new to that clade, such as bipedality in hominins, the clade that consists of primates more closely related to humans than to any other living primate. In Figure 2.4 we see the clade of the hominoids, the apes, is partly characterized by the derived trait of not having a tail, compared to the other nonhuman primates.

Moreover, when looking at shared structures in two different groups we need to determine if they are similar because they were inherited from a common ancestor (called **homologies**) or if the features have separate evolutionary origins but are superficially similar (**analogies**). Analogies occur because species may have experienced similar pressures and found similar solutions (such as wings in a bat and in a bird). Homologies, meanwhile, can look similar but have different functions (some inner ear bones in mammals come from ancestral fish jaw bones). If you have ever looked at the hands of a panda or a mole you might have been perplexed by the presence of what looks like a thumb. While it is technically a wrist bone that has been enlarged, both species found a way to adapt to their niche. **Convergent evolution** occurs when organisms who are not closely related independently evolve similar traits to adapt to similar conditions or needs.

SUMMARY

This chapter introduced a lot of complex terminology. To put this into perspective let's examine how diet intersects with genetics. Fava bean crostini with pecorino cheese is a favorite dish for many Italians. But for some of them it can be deadly. The reason for this is a mutation in a gene on the X chromosome that produces a protein known as G6PD. The function of this protein is to protect blood cells from a specific type of stress that occurs when antioxidant levels are low. If antioxidant levels get too low this can cause serious damage to the cells in your body. G6PD helps to protect your red blood cells from oxidative stress.

But fava beans are sources of oxidant stress. Most people have enough copies of the G6PD protein and can respond to this nutritional stress effectively. But some have a mutation in this gene which means they have a harder time coping with this stress. Known as favism, this condition affects about 400 million people worldwide. In some it can cause anemia, jaundice, heart failure, and even death. Interestingly, a specific Mediterranean variant, known as G6PD Med, seems to protect against a form of malaria, which may explain why it is so prevalent in some regions.

While the mechanisms behind favism have only been learned recently, the fact that we inherit traits from our biological parents and that, because of that, we have a tendency to look and maybe behave in similar ways is not new. But understanding why this happens at the genetic level is integral to understanding the causes of human variation, a topic we will examine in depth in the next chapter.

1. DNA is often said to be a blueprint but in fact it is more complex than that. The genetic code tells a cell what amino acids to link together to make proteins, but this happens within a

whole developmental system that involves other genes and the organisms environment.

2. Heritability is the amount of phenotypic variation that can be explained by genotypic variation within a specific population and environment. When scientists say a trait is heritable they are describing how much variation in that trait is due to genetics within a specific group.

3. Biological evolution can be defined as change in allele frequency from one generation to another. The forces of evolution affect these frequencies and we can look for deviation from Hardy–Weinberg equilibrium to find examples of biological evolution.

4. Speciation is often the result of natural selection acting on a population that has been split into two due to geographic or behavioral barriers.

5. Studying adaptations requires knowledge of the different ways in which a species can develop traits.

FURTHER READING

Banks, Martin S., William W. Sprague, Jürgen Schmoll, Jared A. Q. Parnell, and Gordon D. Love. 2015. Why Do Animal Eyes Have Pupils of Different Shapes? *Science Advances* 1(7): e1500391. https://doi.org /sciadv.1500391. *An interesting paper that looks at the adaptations in different pupil shapes in animals. Not necessarily anthropological but a good example of how to apply evolutionary thinking to different phenotypes.*

Diegues, Andreia, Pedro Simões, Tiago Ceriz, Ana Rita Lopes, and Elisa Tomé. 2022. Favism: A Case Report. *Cureus* 14(3): e23269. https://doi.org /10.7759/cureus.23269. *Overview of favism and its effects on cultural evolution.*

Fairbanks, Daniel. 2022. *Gregor Mendel: His Life and Legacy Hardcover*. Prometheus. *Very interesting biography of Gregor Mendel and his work.*

Gillespie, John H. 2004. *Population Genetics: A Concise Guide*. Johns Hopkins University Press. *A really good overview on population genetics. A bit easier to read than the Falconer volume (below), and after reading this you will know a lot about how populations evolve.*

Falconer, Douglas S. 1996. *Introduction to Quantitative Genetics*. Benjamin Cummings. *A classic book on genetics that is heavy on the mathematical aspects of genomics. If you want to learn more about modern genetics this book is a great place to start.*

Lasisi, Tina, James W. Smallcombe, W. Larry Kenney, Mark D. Shriver, Benjamin Zydney, Nina G. Jablonski, and George Havenith. 2023. Human Scalp Hair as a Thermoregulatory Adaptation. *Proceedings of the National Academy of Sciences* 120(24): e2301760120. https://doi.org/10.1073/pnas.2301760120. *Examines the evolution of human scalp hair showing that tightly curled hair provides effective protection for the scalp against solar radiation, while minimizing the need for sweat.*

McDonald, John. 2012. https://udel.edu/~mcdonald/mythintro.html. *McDonald's website is a wonderful resource for looking at myths of human genetics. I highly recommend checking it out.*

Poczai, Péter, Neil Bell, and Jaakko Hyvönen. 2014. Imre Festetics and the Sheep Breeders' Society of Moravia: Mendel's Forgotten 'Research Network.' *PLOS Biology* 12(1): e1001772. https://doi.org/10.1371/journal.pbio.1001772. *One of the few sources on the life of Imre Festetics. Interesting because his work is often ignored in overviews of the history of genetics.*

Sacks, Oliver. 1998. *The Island of the Colorblind.* Vintage. *More on the effect of the typhoon hit the island of Pingelap in Micronesia. And an overall fascinating book to read.*

Segal, Nancy. 2021. *Deliberately Divided: Inside the Controversial Study of Twins and Triplets Adopted Apart.* Rowman & Littlefield Publishers. *If you want to learn more about scientists have studied heritability, and some of the controversial aspects of that work, this book is eye opening.*

Vitzthum, Virginia J. 2003. A Number No Greater than the Sum of Its Parts: The Use and Abuse of Heritability. *Human Biology* 75(4): 539–558. https://doi.org/10.1353/hub.2003.0064. *Good and concise overview of heritability.*

3

HUMAN BIOLOGY

CHAPTER OVERVIEW

Knowing the processes that occur at the molecular level that create variation is only one part of how biological anthropologists begin to understand the causes of variation in humans today and in the past. We also need to understand what happens at the level of populations. To answer these questions, we can turn to another subfield of bioanthropology: human biology.

Human biologists study variation in biological traits such as adaptations, life history, population dynamics, health outcomes, and heredity. They examine these traits among, within, and between human populations to understand the origin and maintenance of these variables.

An important concept in this chapter is **embodiment**, which examines how we incorporate the material and social worlds we live in into our biology. No aspect of our biology can be understood absent knowledge of our history, in terms of both our ancestry and our own lived experiences.

In this chapter we will look at our biology in the light of evolution. We will start by thinking about what sorts of pressures different species face and how they can respond to them. Then we will examine how humans grow up and become adults, using this to think about what it tells us about human evolution. After building up these tools we examine two types of variation in humans that have receive a lot of attention: biological sex and race.

DOI: 10.4324/9781003390442-4

PRESSURE

As living beings our bodies are exposed to outside pressures. These pressures come from the environment we live in, such as heat and cold, and social stressors, such as living in groups with others. Animals need to be able to respond to extreme conditions such as radiation from the sun, stress from lack of nutrition, high altitude living, and dealing with extreme temperatures. Anthropologist Roberto Frisancho suggested that we can examine how a species respond to pressure in three different but intersecting ways: **Accommodations**, **adaptations**, and **acclimatizations**.

Accommodations are cultural or behavioral modifications to fit the environment. An acclimatization is a developmental or physiological change to fit the environment, such as a young child responding to moving to a higher altitude by having their lungs grow larger so they can get more oxygen. Adaptations, as discussed in the last chapter, describe when biological evolution occurs to better fit the environment.

Many species use behavioral modifications. For example, young bottlenose dolphins are taught to use sponges to forage the seabed for food. In humans, accommodations are often cultural in nature, meaning that they are transmitted non-genetically. Culture is one of the central concepts of anthropology but also notoriously difficult to define. Anthropologists debate how common culture is in other species, but many believe it is not limited to humans. A simple definition is that culture is learned behavior that is transmitted from one individual to another.

Humans possess sophisticated cultural systems that help us adjust to the environment. Importantly, these cultural accommodations affect natural selection's impact on us. A million years ago having an impacted molar would most likely lead to death, but today for people with access to healthcare it means a trip to the dentist. Accommodations allow humans to respond to pressure without needing to adapt or acclimate, letting us inhabit new areas and climates much more quickly without having to wait for biological evolution.

One of the most common types of pressure humans and other organisms need to respond to is the climate. As humans explore and inhabit regions of the Earth with different climatic zones, we need to find ways to deal with extreme heat, intense cold, and high altitude environments. Different types of adaptations, accommodations, and acclimatizations exist that allow us to be a global species.

Heat can cause many problems. Adaptations to heat include vasodilation, which increases the blood flow to the surface tissues under the skin. Since the blood is closer to the surface, this results in more heat loss, cooling us down at times of intense heat. Sweating, which cools the skin, is another human adaptation. Here, the brain signals the sweat glands to produce sweat, which appear on the surface of the skin. Energy is drawn away as the water is vaporized, cooling the body down. On the other hand, vasoconstriction and an increased basal metabolic rate help to keep us warm in colder climates.

Other adaptations to climate are seen in a species overall body size and shape. Probably the most famous of these in the biology world are ecological laws known as **Bergmann's rule** and **Allen's rule**. Bergmann's rule states that species in colder regions will be more massive than those in warmer regions because larger animals have a lower surface area to volume ratio. This lower ratio means they lose relatively less heat than a smaller animal would. For example, polar bears are larger than brown bears as the former are adapted to the arctic temperatures.

Allen's rule discusses the relationship between the length of an animals' appendages and temperature. Mammals in cold climates have shorter appendages compared to comparable animals in warmer climates. Having short limbs means they can keep warm at the core around their vital organs. Again, this is because there is less surface area for heat loss. This is why arctic hares have short ears compared to jackrabbits who live in the desert. It is possible that elephants have such large ears in order to help dissipate heat as well.

These rules are difficult to understand. The important aspect is how heat loss is related to surface size. I like my colleague Libby Cowgill's example of how waffles cool down quicker than pancakes. As waffles have all the nooks in them, a waffle has a larger surface area even though it is roughly the same size as a pancake.

Another geographically related ecology rule that is of interest to anthropologists is the island rule (also called 'Foster's rule').

This rule states that animals can evolve to be bigger or smaller in response to resource availability. The best-known example of this may be pygmy mammoths. These mammoths used to live off on an island of the coast of California. Insular dwarfism reduced their body size 20% the size of mammoths from the mainland. In other species, we see the opposite happening, with insular gigantism increasing the size of a species such as giant rodents and the (sadly extinct) gorilla-sized lemurs of Madagascar.

Pressure also comes from living at high altitude, where the main problem is **hypoxia**, a lack of oxygen. The higher up one goes the harder it is to obtain oxygen from the atmosphere. It also tends to be colder and there is less biodiversity at high altitude as well. Above 2,500 meters (8,200 ft) humans need either accommodations, adaptations, or acclimatizations to prevent high altitude sickness and hypoxia.

A person born at sea-level who travels above 2,500 meters can slowly acclimatize to the lack of available oxygen by producing more red blood cells. Such acclimatizations let their body take in and transport more oxygen. However, these changes would dissipate when they went back to a lower altitude. Cultural accommodations such as higher carbohydrate diets have also allowed humans to live in these regions. And for people who are not native to the region, accommodations allow them to visit these regions, such as mountain climbers bringing oxygen with them to avoid mountain sickness.

There have also been some adaptations to high altitude living. Humans have been living on the Tibetan Plateau, which is about 4,000 meters (13,100 ft) above sea level, since at least 40,000 years ago (though might not have had a permanent presence until 5,000 years ago). Biological adaptations here include having wider blood vessels and an increased breath rate, both of which allows for better oxygenation of the body. Meanwhile in the Andes Mountain range in South America, groups have increased the volume of their red blood cells and have more hemoglobin.

Other adaptations in human evolutionary history revolve around our diet and nutrition. The agricultural revolution began when humans started to grow their own food rather than gather and hunt. This changed our diets to a remarkable extent. Many people growing up in the US have heard the slogan 'Milk does a body good' and have been raised to think that we should drink lots of milk. But the alleles that let humans digest lactose post-weaning are recent in evolutionary terms, arising after 10,000 years ago. In fact, many people today cannot drink milk without medications. It is surprising, then, to think that we have called those people out as being lactose intolerant as if that is the ancestral condition that should be fixed. From an anthropological standpoint those of us who can drink milk are the mutants.

It is not always obvious or easy to separate the three types of responses to stress. The important lesson is that understanding why certain traits exist often requires evolutionary thinking. Applying these ideas to humans is never easy and often controversial due to the complications of humans as the products of biology and culture.

A great example of this comes in the next section, where we look at the evolutionary conundrum of why it takes humans so long to become adults (or, put in a different way, why we are so helpless for so long).

LIFE HISTORY

Life history theory explores how an organism allocates the limited resources at its disposal. Often times, this involves researching the tradeoffs that exist between different developmental processes. Living things must balance two different needs: developmental growth and reproduction. Questions such as why some species have many offspring while others only have a few, or why some species take a long time to become adults and others reach sexual maturity quickly are examined by looking at the costs and benefits for an organism in its environment and seeing how these can be optimized.

Mortality and fecundity are two important traits here. In order to do study theses, we separate out **extrinsic** and **intrinsic** factors. Extrinsic factors are outside pressures such as the environment while intrinsic ones are constraints at the biological level, such as age or disease.

Life history is about with hedging bets and dealing with risk. For example, becoming an adult quickly (i.e., having a short maturation time) is often beneficial since you spend less time as an easily predated creature. However, growing up quickly means you have a smaller adult body size than a species that grows slowly. A longer maturation means a larger body, and a larger body size is associated with higher fecundity.

In other words, if you take time to grow up, you run the risk of not making it to adulthood. But a longer time spent as a juvenile means you have more time to learn and might be a better adult/ parent. Because of this, organisms allocate resources in different ways at different life stages.

Anthropologists can look at the sequence and timing of major events in an organism's lifetime to better understand their evolution and biology. Like body size and tooth morphology, life history is an adaptive character. As one of the goals of evolution is to maximize reproduction, examining how a species allocates its resources over its lifespan can tell us about a species' evolutionary history. Studying life history can clue us into aspects of evolution

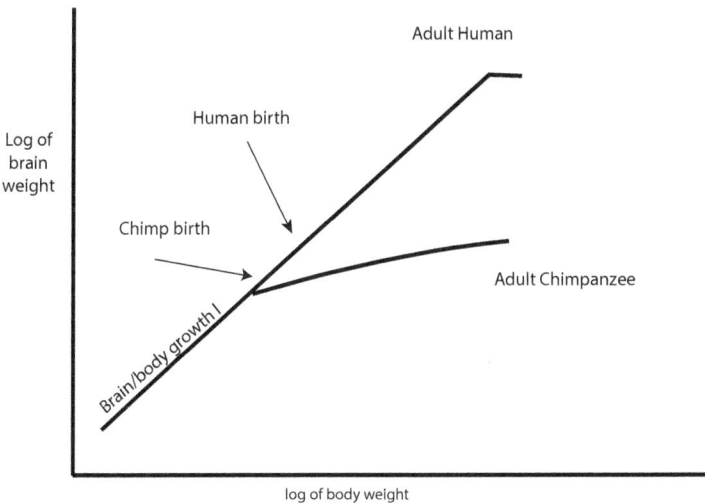

Figure 3.1 Growth curve for human brain and body compared with that of a chimpanzee.

Image based on figure 5 from Barry Bogin, and B. Holly Smith, "Evolution of the human life cycle," American Journal of Human Biology 8.6 (1996): 703–716

and on the extrinsic and intrinsic pressures our ancestors faced. The fact that it takes humans a long time to become sexually mature can be used to understand the types of pressures our ancestors faced.

Humans are known for our odd life history, which includes slow growth during childhood, a long period of infant dependency, and delayed reproduction. From birth to reproductive maturity, contemporary human growth and development is characterized by five stages: infancy, childhood, juvenile, adolescence, and adulthood.

If you have ever been a caregiver for a baby or a young child, you know how helpless (but cute!) they can be. The fact that it takes humans such a long time to be able to take care of themselves and then to reproduce is confusing from an evolutionary perspective. Perhaps by growing slow we learn the skills to be more successful adults. In this section we apply evolutionary thinking to understand why new life stages evolve.

From a parent's evolutionary perspective, parenthood involves maximizing the number of children who can survive long enough to reproduce themselves. When a mother has a fetus inside of her she is, in some sense, dealing with a parasite. For the birthing mother, having the fetus born as soon as possible is better as it frees her to have another child or to simply allocate energy in a different way. But from the fetus's perspective, being in utero for as long as possible is advantageous. Parent–offspring conflict is more common than you may think. Baboon mothers often fight with their young kids who, while too heavy to still carry, complain when their mom makes them walk on their own.

When we are born we are more underdeveloped, and more dependent on parental care, than most mammals. When chimpanzees are born, their brains are about 37% the size they will be as an adult. But for humans, that number is closer to 25%. In other words, while a baby's brain is massive it still has much more to grow relative to other mammals. Some have argued that humans are born 'early' due to the necessity of fitting a large brain through the birth canal. There are different (and antagonistic) forces acting on a mother's pelvis and a fetus's brain.

The **obstetric dilemma** looks at the conflict between the need for a spacious birth canal and the keeping the pelvis narrow, which helps make bipedal locomotion more efficient. This theory suggests that humans are born immature as an evolutionary solution to this dilemma. Scholars have also pointed out that while active assistance in birth is common in humans, it is rare in non-human primates.

Others question the legitimacy of the obstetric dilemma hypothesis. They note that it assumes that women walk less efficiently than men due to their pelvic shape and that humans are born early. For these scholars, it is not the shape of the baby's head that matters but rather the energy cost to the mother.

Either way, infants are reliant on others for food (for mammals this is usually through breastfeeding). For many mammals, as soon as they are weaned they are on their own. Social mammals, however, evolved what is known as the juvenile period, a time when they are no longer reliant on mother's milk and can obtain food on their own.

This juvenile period is a time of slow growth. As with other stages, it must have some function, since otherwise it is dangerous to being small and not being able to scare away competitors or predators. Since the juvenile period is often observed in mammals that live in groups, it may be that the juvenile period is correlated with learning and growth. Slow juvenile growth reduces the risk of death and provides time to learn how to be a better adult.

Humans, at some point in our evolutionary history, evolved a stage between juvenile and infancy. This is our childhood, a period following weaning when the youngster is still dependent on others for food and protection. This assistance does not have to come from a biological parent. Instead, other adults or older siblings can help the child.

This **alloparenting** frees a parent to put energy into another offspring. **Cooperative breeding** occurs where females in a group do not all breed regularly but provide alloparent care to the offspring of a breeding females. As we will see in Chapter 4, nonhuman primates care for their young in complex ways.

Childcare evolved to help spread responsibly. It allows caregiving behavior in other individuals, such as babysitting children who are not your own. Childhood also allows the growing child to react to internal or external environmental factors by acclimating via a change in their movement or rate of activity, a process known as **developmental plasticity**. The fact that we view kids as cute and adorable makes sense from an evolutionary perspective: natural selection produced a feeling of wanting to care for them based on their cuteness.

Adolescence is a transition period from juvenile to adulthood. Humans have a relatively long adolescence. As we reach puberty, we need to focus on both maintenance, growth, and reproduction, something that is difficult. There is a shift from a focus on maintenance and growth to a focus on maintenance and reproduction. The relatively long time it takes to grow up allows humans to learn the social skills necessary to be an effective parent (or simply an effective adult).

Adulthood is a time of a lot of stress and risk, but also the potential to increase fitness by passing on genes to the next generation. In many human cultures, adulthood is the time of marriage and children. For contemporary humans this is often a time of learning as well. Humans seem unique in that we can be biologically mature but still not considered to be adults by our own culture.

A significant part of life history for half the world during adulthood is menstruation, the shedding of the lining of the uterus that happens monthly. As anthropologist Kate Clancy shows in her book *Period*, menstruation has been understudied and misunderstood by science. Her cultural history delves into the myths and assumptions about periods, noting that it is unclear why menstruation exists and if periods have an adaptive function.

Menopause, the stage of life when a woman's menstrual period stops, is also evolutionarily interesting. This has received a lot of attention since few species other than humans seem to have a postmenopause life. Recent findings suggest that both female whales and chimps can live for a long time after they are no longer fertile. While it is not clear why menopause evolved, perhaps there is a greater overall fitness benefit in putting energy towards the group they live in rather than in having their own kids. As one gets older and nears the end of life it becomes more likely that they will not live long enough to care for their children. Instead of having a child at seventy, and maybe not surviving past the child's adolescence, a parent can put their energy towards the grandkids (or other group members).

While it is inevitable, we often try to avoid thinking about death. But from a biological standpoint it is interesting to think about why this occurs. From one perspective, it might seem that living forever would allow an organism to pass on more genes. If that is the case, why hasn't such a system evolved? One reason might be that some genes are good early in life but then bad later in life. Having an increased reproductive output and large body size might allow an organism to pass on its genes at its peak, but then become deleterious later. This theory, called the antagonistic pleiotropy hypothesis, is supported by some work on testosterone levels.

As an adaptive trait, life history provides biological anthropologists with information and theories as to what happened in the past. The 15 or so years it takes humans to reach reproductive maturity gives contemporary humans the ability to learn how to be better adults, and that provides a higher fitness overall.

Life history theory reminds us of the power of evolutionary thinking to understand why traits exist. At the same time, it is important to realize that the evolutionary reasons for a trait or characteristic does not assign a cultural value to that trait. Just because we might know why a trait evolved does not take away its meaning to us.

SEX AND GENDER

Human biology is grounded in the concept that humans are biocultural, a concept that sees biological and cultural evolution as interrelated. An anthropologists might be asked to explain why in some cultures boys are dressed in blue and girls dressed in pink. Is there a biological reason for this observation? One hypothesis could argue that there are innate differences or evolved reasons for these color preferences. Perhaps this division goes back to our distant past as foragers and is based on a sexual division of labor. Another hypothesis, however, could point to cultural reasons and historical practices, such as companies recognizing that selling products based on gender means that they can sell more items. In fact, it seems that marketing influenced this divide, with the idea that boys should wear blue clothes and that girls should wear pink becoming more common after the 1950s.

In 1843, a town in the US state of Connecticut was getting ready for an election. The Whig party, hoping to win a close election, presented members to the town board in order to have them approved as voters (at the time, only free men who owned property were allowed to vote). One of these people was Levi Suydam. Suydam was approved to vote by the board and cast a ballot. But this was a close election, with a party winning by just one vote! The other side contested the election on the grounds that Suydam was not male.

When first inspected by town doctors, one group argued he was a man since he had a penis. But the doctor who reported the case noted that Suydam 'was more a female than a male, and that, in his physical organization, he partook of both sexes.' Suydam's sister said that he menstruated (she was the one who washed his laundry). The same doctor who argued he was a man reexamined Suydam and noted other characteristics such as Suydam being 'every way of a feminine figure.' He also had 'an aversion for bodily labor, and an inability to perform the same.' The doctor seemed to change his mind once he heard about aspects of Suydam's behaviors rather than anything physical.

Suydam's story reminds us that our categories rarely map perfectly onto our biology. In this section we look at how biological anthropologists approach sex and gender. We will learn that it is not easy, and might be impossible, to fully disentangle the two. Sex differentiation during fetal development can help us to understand the complex set of steps that happens. We will also look at examples of how differences of sex development inform the question of human variation. Claims that there are only two sexes oversimplifies the biological and social world.

Biological sex is often defined at birth. In many societies this is assigned by a medical professional based on a baby's genitalia, a vagina or penis. But biological sex includes both the biological and physiological characteristics that are used to define males and females such as chromosomes and hormone levels. Many scientists define sex by the gametes that an individual produces: in mammals, females make large ones (eggs) and males make small ones (sperm). Technically speaking, females make all their eggs before they are born. A fetus will create all the eggs they will use in their lifetime by around twenty weeks. What that means is that someone who is growing a fetus has the eggs in them that could become that parent's future grandchild.

Gender, meanwhile, is the socially constructed roles, behaviors, activities, and attributes that a given society considers appropriate for men and women. As this is socially determined, gender norms are based on where and when we grow up. Behaviors deemed 'acceptable' by a society now might have been considered 'wrong' in the recent past as cultural norms change.

While the above might seem easy enough to follow, it will not surprise you by now to learn that biological sex is much more complex. Female spider monkeys have what is sometimes called a 'pseudo-penis,' which is a large clitoris. This is also seen female fossa, a cat-like species found in Madagascar.

Gender, too, is complicated, with many cultures having more than two gender categories. Sometimes referred to as 'third gen-der,' these people are seen as neither men nor women but often a mix or blend of the two, filling a role between male and female. Hijras, mahu, muxes, two-spirits, and fa'afafines are just some examples of third genders in different cultures.

Examples like Levi Suydam's attempt to vote stress both the importance and limitation of definitions. The ways scholars define categories affects how we classify group members. For that reason, some have suggested using the phrasing sex/gender, which empha-sizes the biological and social intersections and entanglements of sex and gender. While more complicated than many would like, sex/gender reminds us that we cannot separate biology and culture.

The statistical distribution of a trait in a human population co-exists with a distribution of ideas about what we think constitutes a 'normal' version of that trait. Cultural norms inform develop-ment of research questions, data collection, analysis and interpre-tations. It was not until fairly recently that the US used crash-test dummies that had muscle-mass and proportions that were based on women, which might explain why women are more likely than men to be seriously injured in a car crash. Transgender (umbrella term for people whose gender identity and /or gender expression differs from what is associated with the sex they were assigned at birth) and non-binary (identities that are somewhere between or outside of the gender binary) individuals have largely been ignored in psychological research.

Given all of this, we can see the difficulty with the idea that gender is a culturally constructed social experience and sex is the biological characteristic related to reproductive anatomy or physiology. These two cannot be easily separated. Bodies exist on spectrums of difference, and they are far more complex than our categories. Ideas such as what professions are appropriate for each sex are gender norms as well. When trains began to travel over 50 miles an hour, some people suggested that women should not be allowed on them, since going at that speed would mean that their uteruses would fly out of their bodies!

To better understand sex/gender we need to explore what is happening biologically when a sexually indifferent embryo begins to acquire male or female. This process, known as sex differentiation, is very complex. Biological sex is determined as the fetus grows. Fetuses look identical until sixth week of gestation, at which time sex differentiation begins. Before that time everyone has the same ducts and gonad tissue. Male and female characteristics begin to show with the development of gonads and external genitalia.

Most biology textbooks will tell you that the fetus will develop along the female typical path unless it receives a certain signal. This signal comes from a gene on the Y chromosome called the SRY gene, which produces the SRY protein. The SRY protein is the first step in the development of the testes. It causes the bipotential gonads to become the testes, which in turn produces testosterone. This testosterone signals the creation and development of the rest of male reproductive system. If the fetus does not respond to the SRY protein it will develop along the female typical path.

Because of this, male and female reproductive anatomy are homologous, structures arising from the same tissues. Table 3.1 lists some of the homologous sex organs.

TABLE 3.1 Some of the homologous sex organs in males and females.

Male	Female
Testis	Ovary
Head of the penis	Clitoris
Scrotum	Labia majora

The discussion above suggests that the 'default' pattern is being female. Anthropologist Emily Martin has noted that this implies that being male is the active role. The narrative removes any sort of agency in being female. In fact, the processes of sex determination are much more complex but it might seem like this system means that being female is 'passive' and inert compared to the 'more complex' male system. As Lucy Cooke notes, we should think of the SRY gene not as the sole member of the orchestra but rather as the conductor.

DIFFERENCES IN SEX DEVELOPMENT

Casimir Pulaski was a Polish Revolutionary War hero whose body was thought to buried in Savannah, Georgia. After exhuming the body to test if the skeleton was his, scientists discovered something surprising. While it was very likely his body, the skeleton looked more female than male, especially in the pelvis. Reflecting on this discovery, scholars suggested that Pulaski was intersex, though he might not have known this.

While some argue that chromosomes can be used to tell what someone's sex is, this is not as straightforward as we might think. We use the phrase *differences in sex development* (DSD) to discuss when a person's sex development is different from most other people. It is hard to say how often this occurs, and estimates vary wildly how often someone is born with a combination of physical traits. Importantly, some activists prefer the term intersex to differences in sex development.

There are numerous ways in which the chromosomal makeup of an individual does not match their phenotype. In some cases, an individual's sex chromosomes do not necessarily match their observed sex. As we learned in the last chapter, genes do not always function in the typical way. Mutations in the SRY gene can lead to an allele that does not produce the SRY protein. Other times the Y chromosome is completely missing the SRY gene. If someone is XY with a non-functioning SRY gene they will develop along the female-typical path, though depending upon the exact nature of their mutation they may never undergo puberty without hormone therapy.

In some rare cases during crossing over/recombination, the SRY gene will 'move' to the X chromosomes. In this case, someone who is chromosomally XX but has an SRY gene due to this recombination will develop along the male typical path and be phenotypically male even though they do not have a Y chromosome.

Other ways this can happen include having two X chromosomes and one Y. Or only have one X chromosome and be missing the other sex chromosome. In the latter case phenotypically they are female but will often have delayed sexual development and may not have ovaries.

Jacobs syndrome is a rare condition where an individual has one X chromosome and two Y chromosomes. It is unclear how common this condition is and probable that most people who are XYY are unaware of it. But some early research suggested that men who are XYY are more violent, with the media reports dubbing them 'supermale.' Recent work has questioned this hypothesis. While there is no strong link known between people with Jacobs syndrome and criminal behavior, the theory that they are more violent does provide insight into how *ideas* about genetics and behavior affect our assumptions. Normative notions of what it means to be 'male,' mixed with the idea that a Y chromosome is what drives being a male, made people think they will see a pattern. So much so that some proposed screening men for an extra Y chromosome to help identify potential criminals.

To make things even more complicated, some species have lost their Y chromosome all together! It isn't clear how the Okinawa spiny rat (*Tokudaia osimensis* and *T. Tokunoshimensis*) males are developed but it does show us that nature is never as clear as we think it is.

Beyond chromosomes, there are other DSDs that demonstrate that sex is a spectrum rather than a binary. People with congenital adrenal hyperplasia (CAH) have bodies that do not produce enough corticosteroids. The brain senses this is missing and sends signals to the adrenal glands to try to make more of this hormone. In the process the adrenal glands end up producing more androgens, which are a masculinizing hormone. Females with this condition tend to display masculinized genitalia.

Androgen-insensitivity syndrome (AIS) is a X-linked disorder where some cell receptors are unresponsive to androgens. People who are XY with AIS have 'normal' testosterone levels but the fetus does not masculinize. As a result, their external genitalia are often female but they do not have a uterus.

In 5 alpha reductase deficiency, individuals lack the enzyme that converts testosterone to dihydrotestosterone (DHT), which conducts the development of external genitalia. If no DHT is produced, the person will develop male internal organs but be externally female or ambiguous. However, when puberty hits another jolt of testosterone leads the penis to grow. In one community in the Dominican Republic people with this condition are known as *güevedoces*, which means 'testes at twelve.'

So, what do we know about sex/gender? Biological sex is the product of different levels of activity that begin in utero and continue for decades afterwards. Since biology and culture cannot be separated in humans, it is more accurate to talk about sex-gender and think about the complex patterns of interactions that make a human.

RACE AND RACISM

As discussed briefly in Chapter 1, the history of bioanthropology is intertwined with the history of the study of race. In this section we look at how the ways in which biological anthropologists think about race has changed over time.

Race has multiple definitions. The biological version of the race concept is a framework that hypothesizes that humans are naturally divisible into a small number of reasonably discrete kinds of people. These groups each have distinctive properties that they share with each other. This theory argues that the people within each group have innate biological differences that link them together with each other. Race, in this formulation, is not simply differences, but differences that *matter*. Importantly, the 'scientific' study of race as biology began with a set of conclusions. They argued that races are inherently rankable in biological and behavioral criteria. 'Facts' were gathered to support conclusions, then cited as proof that the original conclusions were true.

In the cultural construct of race, race is a culturally structured, systematic way of looking at, perceiving, and interpreting reality. Race is a social construct, which means that it exists as a result of human interaction. It is the result of many different factors, such as experiences, health, education, economics, political context, physiology, and development. The way race is used today is as a shorthand for several different factors such as ethnic background and social history. Because of this, race changes over time and space and is not static. This is why it is a social construct. When an online form or census asks you what your race is, what it is really asking is how you fit with respect to a system created to organize humanity.

Anthropologists have shown that the biological version does not work. Race is a socially created reality, not an intrinsic reality that has natural demarcations. Or to put it another way, it is artificially drawn by human beings in response to social issues. This means that race is not biology but an idea that we assign to biology. Because social constructs are embodied, the race concept has produced racialized differences, but not for the reasons many initially might believe.

However, it is important to realize that just because race is not biological does not mean it is not very real. Like any other structure, its effects on people are different. The anthropologist insight from decades of research is that race as seen today is the result of racism.

For many years, medical textbooks would explain the observation that Black Americans experience higher rates of hypertension than white Americans is due to the effects of the slave trade. This hypothesis suggested that slave ships acted as a form of selection that led to the descendants of slaves being those whose ancestors were able to retain sodium and thus more likely to survive the passage. The idea that the heritage of slavery is linked to hypertension is, however, not well supported. For example, dehydration and salt depletion were not major causes of death on slave ships and diet is major cause of hypertension. It does show the power of racialized thinking. Why do we turn to genetics rather than social inequality?

Differential outcomes between races exist not between 'racial' genes, but in social institutions and practices. As anthropologist

Jon Marks notes, there are a number of indicators that show that race isn't biology.

1. *The clustering of these groups is arbitrary and based on historical and political ideas rather than scientific ones.*

The definition and association of people with a race has changed over time. The US census in 1790 listed three racial categories; now there are more than 15. Furthermore, your race can change based on where you live, as different countries have different ways of delineating different groups.

Whiteness is the culturally constructed concept in the US that was used to establish boundaries of who was white. For a long time, the United States federal guideline defined 'white' as anyone with origins in Europe, North Africa or the Middle East. This, though, has been critiqued by some people from these regions because they do not see themselves as white.

2. *From a genetic standpoint, there is more genetic variation within groups than between groups.*

Geneticist Richard Lewontin showed that 85% of genetic variation is found *within* human groups rather than *between* them. What this means is that within each major racial group there is more variation than there is between races. A typical region in the human genome is not as differentiated as we might guess from looking at our external features.

This idea is sometimes hard to grasp. To visualize how there can be more variation within a population rather than between populations, picture an American football team. The linesmen who do the blocking are often massive, weighing around 136 kg (300 lb). But the quarterback who throws the ball weights closer to 100 kg (220 lb). In other words, there is a lot of variation in the mass of players within one American football team. But if you compared two teams to each other the variation in the weights will be the same within each group. In Figure 3.2 the mass of the players on the Carolina Panthers is shown, with the median value around 230. But when we compare them to the Arizona Cardinals and other teams in figure 3.3 the variation in weight is

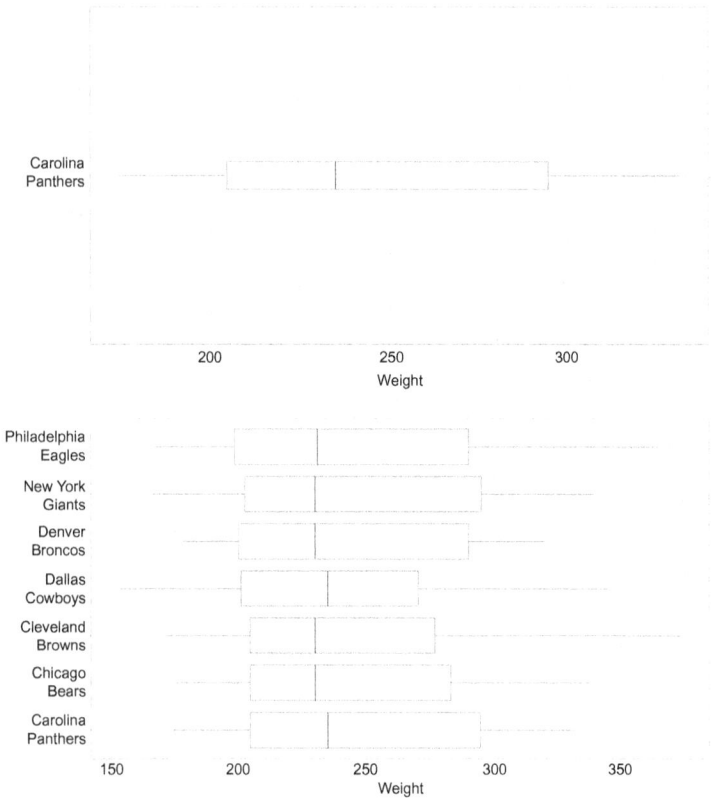

Figure 3.2 (a) Boxplot of the mass of the current players on the Carolina Panthers football team. (b) Boxplot of the mass of the current players on the multiple football team.

Data from https://newsday.sportsdirectinc.com

similar. In other words, there is more weight variation within a team than between teams. This is true of genetic variation within and between populations.

This finding has been confirmed by more recent studies that look at genetic differences among people. A 2025 study of more than 230,000 people showed that most genetic variance is within race and ethnic groups rather than between those groups. These geneticists showed that self-identified race and ethnicity groups have gradients of genetic variation rather than discrete clusters.

Genetic data can see the results of colonization, the transatlantic slave trade, and recent migrations.

This does not imply that classification using multi-locus genomic data is not possible. Lewontin's focus was not on classification overall, but what do our racial classification say about genotypes. There are no characteristics, no traits, not even one gene that turns up in all members of one so-called race yet is absent from others

3. *Human biological variation is continuous, not discrete.*

One of the most obvious human phenotypes is skin color. It is this trait, more than anything else, that has been used to assign people to various racial groups. But it also shows how misleading human variation can be if we look at only one trait. Skin pigmentation is in fact an atypical trait as it does show shows large differences between major continental groups. But it is also a great example of how natural selection works. Skin pigmentation also is a good reminder that human biological variation is continuous, not discrete.

Pigmentation is controlled by melanin, of which there are two types. Pheomelanin produces lighter skin and eumelanin produces darker skin. The more eumelanin in your skin the darker your skin tone. Darkly pigmented skin is more adaptive closer to the equator while lightly pigmented skin is more adaptive further away. The reason for this is because dark skin contains more melanin, which protects against harmful portions of ultraviolet (UV) radiation. But UV radiation is not equal across the globe and it is higher closer to the equator. This is because sunlight passes through a less thick atmosphere at those points. In places with higher UV radiation having darkly pigmented skin makes evolutionary sense.

However, another type of UV radiation from the sun allows for the synthesis of vitamin D. Since UV radiation decreases as one moves away from the equator, people with a lot of melanin have a harder time receiving enough UV radiation to process vitamin D. For people who live in these northern regions natural selection has relaxed the selection on dark skin and at the same time selected for lighter skin in northern latitudes to allow for the synthesis of vitamin D.

To summarize this section, racial issues are social-political-economic, not biological. But race has significant real-world effects since racialized inequalities affect us. The embodiment of racism is what produces what we see as race. As cultural beings we incorporate the material/social world in which we live into our biology. As anthropologist Lance Gravlee noted health inequalities exist between racial groups not because race is inherently real but because social inequalities shape the biology of racialized groups.

Experiencing unfair treatment due to one's racial background leads to high blood pressure, cancer, low birth rate, and depression. Embodiment, how we incorporate the material and social world in which we live into our biology, affects us in many ways and no aspect of our biology can be understood absent knowledge of our history.

CHAPTER SUMMARY

As the descendants of primates who were constantly on guard for predators, much of our biology is attuned to being on the alert. Human biologists use these ideas to think on how the constant stress placed on contemporary humans affects us at a biological level. Being attuned to potentially threatening stressors is helpful from an evolutionary perspective.

This section explores some of the most relevant questions people have about why and how humans look the way they do. Human biologists can use their expertise to help shape public policy and health care issues. It allows us to better assess the implications of these variations. A major theme of twenty-first-century bioanthropology is that no aspect of our biology can be understood absent knowledge of history. Being characterized affects you immensely. Differential outcomes between races exist not between 'racial' genes, but in social institutions and practices. As mentioned above, the practice of racism produces the illusion of race, what Karen and Barbara Fields call *Racecraft*.

This chapter looked at how we can understand the variation in biological traits among and within human populations. By thinking about these differences, we not only can better understand how evolution affected us, but also push back against racist, sexist, and other problematic ways of conceptualizing that patterns seen in contemporary humans.

The major takeaway from human biology is that the idea that biological things are 'real' and cultural things are 'social' is way too simplistic. Work in bioanthropology and related fields have shown that much of what we think about the ways in which we can organize human groups is shaped by cultural biases.

1. Organisms need to find ways to respond to the pressures placed on them by solar radiation, high altitude living, extreme temperatures and other factors. Accommodation, adaptation, and acclimatization are three ways in which responses occur.
2. Life history theory looks at the sequence and timing of major events in an organism's lifespan. By looking at this through an evolutionary lens we can understand what sorts of pressures our ancestors faced and how they responded to them.
3. Thinking about sex/gender as intertwined concepts which cannot be easily separated is a better way to think about humans as a biocultural species.
4. The way race is conceptualized today is a poor way of thinking about human biological diversity.
5. The idea that biological things are 'real' and cultural things are 'social' is too simplistic.

FURTHER READING

Benn Torres, Jada, and Gabriel Torres Colón. 2020. *Genetic Ancestry*. Routledge. *An anthropological geneticist and a cultural anthropologist explore what genetic ancestry means.*

Clancy, Kathryn B. H. 2023. *Period*. Princeton University Press. *Written by a biological anthropologist, this book looks at the science and culture of menstruation.*

Cooke, Lucy. 2022. *Bitch: On the Female of the Species*. Basic Books. *A witty and engaging book that shows just how often female bodies have been ignored by science.*

Dunsworth, Holly M., Anna G. Warrener, Terrence Deacon, Peter T. Ellison, and Herman Pontzer. 2012. Metabolic Hypothesis for Human Altriciality. *Proceedings of the National Academy of Sciences* 109(38): 15,212–15,216. https://doi.org/10.1073/pnas.1205282109. *A piece that suggests that anthropologists need to rethink the obstetric dilemma hypothesis.*

Fields, Karen E., and Barbara J. Fields. 2014. *Racecraft: The Soul of Inequality in American Life.* Verso. *A cultural perspective on what race is and what it is not.*

Frisancho, Roberto. 1993. *Human Adaptation and Accommodation.* University of Michigan Press. *A classic book that looks at how humans have responded to pressure.*

Fuentes, Agustín. 2025. *Sex Is a Spectrum: The Biological Limits of the Binary.* Princeton University Press. *How biologists have come to understand that the binary view of sex does not work.*

Gravlee, Clarence C. 2009. How Race Becomes Biology: Embodiment of Social Inequality. *American Journal of Physical Anthropology* 139(1): 47–57. https://doi.org/10.1002/ajpa.20983. *A nuanced look at what it means when anthropologists say race becomes biology.*

Hrdy, Sarah. 2009. *Mothers and Others The Evolutionary Origins of Mutual Understanding.* Harvard University Press. *An anthropological look at childhood, alloparenting and the human capacity for understanding others.*

Hyde, Janet Shibley, Rebecca S. Bigler, Daphna Joel, Charlotte Chucky Tate, and Sari M. van Anders. 2019. The Future of Sex and Gender in Psychology: Five Challenges to the Gender Binary. *The American Psychologist* 74(2): 171–193. https://doi.org/10.1037/amp0000307. *A look at how to push back on the idea of a sex and gender binary.*

Jablonski, Nina G. 2004. The Evolution of Human Skin and Skin Color. *Annual Review of Anthropology* 33(1): 585–623. https://doi.org/10.1146/annurev.anthro.33.070203.143955. *A paper that looks at the evolution of human skin pigmentation by the scholar who figured out much of the natural selection behind this trait.*

Lewontin, R. C. 1972. The Apportionment of Human Diversity. *Evolutionary Biology* 6: 381–398. *More mathematical than many other readings, but the classic paper that showed how genetic variation is partitioned.*

Marks, Jonathan. 2002. *What Does It Mean to Be 98% Chimpanzee?* University of California Press. *A funny and engaging look at bioanthropology.*

Martin, Emily. 1991. The Egg and the Sperm: How Science Has Constructed a Romance Based on Stereotypical Male–Female Roles. *Signs* 16(3): 485–501. *Another classic piece that looks at the ways in which textbooks affect how we view sex determination.*

Roseman, Charles, and Cara Ocobock. 2023. To Understand Sex, We Need to Ask the Right Questions. *Scientific American*, October 24. Retrieved from www.scientificamerican.com/article/to-understand-sex-we-need-to-ask-the-right-questions. *Two anthropologists write on the context of asking how many sexes there are.*

Reiches, Meredith W. 2019. Adolescence as a Biocultural Life History Transition. *Annual Review of Anthropology* 48(1): 151–168. https://doi.org/10.1146/annurev-anthro-102218-011118. *More info on the topic of human life history.*

Reis, Elizabeth. 2005. Impossible Hermaphrodites: Intersex in America, 1620–1960. *Journal of American History* 92(2): 411–441. https://doi.org/10 .2307/3659273. *Looks at the story of Levi Suydam.*

Stearns, Stephen C. 2000. Life History Evolution: Successes, Limitations, and Prospects. *Naturwissenschaften* 87 (11): 476–486. https://doi.org/10 .1007/s001140050763. *Another overview on human life history traits.*

Zhang, X. L., et al. 2018. The Earliest Human Occupation of the High-Altitude Tibetan Plateau 40 Thousand to 30 Thousand Years Ago. *Science* 362(6418): 1049–1051. https://doi.org/10.1126/science.aat8824. *Example of the kind of work done to understand human adaptation.*

4

PRIMATOLOGY

CHAPTER OVERVIEW

The order Primates consists of around 500 different species. Though the exact number of primate species fluctuates and changes with genetic research and new discoveries, primates represent a wide range of sizes, shapes, and ecological adaptations. The world's smallest primate is a mouse lemur, a 30 gram species from Madagascar that can fit in the palm of your hand. Meanwhile the largest extant, or living, primate is a species of gorilla, of which the males can be around 250 kg (a fossil ape known as Gigantopithecus may have been twice the size of a male gorilla). Some primates live in tropical rainforests and others adapted to the desert environment. Japanese macaques live in snowy regions of northern Japan, while some baboons live in South Africa. Some are adapted to live in the trees and rarely leave while others spend their whole lives on the ground.

In the 1960s, Louis Leakey, who was then one of the world's most prominent experts in human evolution, received a message from a colleague who had reported that chimpanzees were using a blade of grass as a tool to 'fish' for termites. He sent back a message back: 'Now we must redefine tool, redefine Man, or accept chimpanzees as humans.' That woman, Jane Goodall (1934–2025), would go on to become the world's most famous primatologist. Before the 1960s, it was common for Western scientists to believe that only humans used tools. But primatology (and studies of other animals) has pushed back on this idea. This chapter introduces the topic of primate variation and diversity. As with other chapters in

DOI: 10.4324/9781003390442-5

this book, we can only skim the surface of what is known about the nonhuman primates.

WHAT IS A PRIMATE?

Partly because we are primates, much work has been put into describing primate anatomy and behavior. Since they are such a diverse group, it is difficult to find traits common to all primates, but they tend to very social, live in groups, have a wide diet, and many are adapted to a life in the trees.

Table 4.1 lists some of the common traits seen in many primates. While there is a lot of variation amongst the primates, some features, both behavioral and anatomical, reflect their evolutionary history. The visual predation hypothesis is based on the concept of **competitive exclusion**, which says that no two species will occupy the same niche. This theory suggests that many generalized features in primates are a reflection of a mammalian ancestor that lived on the ground and ate insects. This mammal had a diet based on eating insects. As an insectivore, it evolved grasping hands to capture prey, losing its claws since that made it difficult to hold onto the insects. They also developed depth perception to aid in capturing insects. Then, by moving into the trees, primate ancestors were able to access a new niche, with the hands and eyes pre-adapted to arboreal life. The visual-predation hypothesis suggests that features shared by primitive primates reflect such an ancestry.

Another theory sees primates as adapting to a diet of flowering plants rather than insects. Called the angiosperm–primate

TABLE 4.1 Some of the common traits seen in primates.

Trait	comments
Arboreal	Adapted to life in the trees—arboreal adaptation in a set of behaviors and anatomical characteristics
Primates eat a wide variety of foods	Dietary plasticity seen in their teeth and jaws
Parental investment	Primates invest a lot of time and care in few offspring

coevolution hypothesis, it suggests that the eating of fruits, seeds, and other parts of flowering plants was integral to the evolution of primates. This hypothesis notes that fruit tend to be at the end of tree branches. To access these foods, primate ancestors needed to develop an ability to hold onto those branches while also being able to spot them in the tree. This model relies on the idea of coevolution. Coevolutionary relationships occur when two species affect each other's evolution, such as the relationship between hummingbirds and specific flowers, where the flower will bloom during the bird's breeding seasons. Intriguingly, this angiosperm-primate coevolution model fits well with what we know about the origins of primates and the origin of fruiting plants, suggesting a coevolution around 50 million years ago.

It is likely that these two hypotheses are not mutually exclusive. Primate origins are complex, but there does seem to be a link between their arboreal nature, their diet, and their novel adaptations.

PRIMATES AS THE 'VISUAL ORDER'

Primates are sometimes referred to as the **visual order**. Unlike many other mammals, they do not rely much on sense of smell. Instead, most primates, except for some of the most primitive ones, have evolved to use sight to find mates and search for food. Because of this, there are many adaptations towards visual acuity, with some primates evolving distinctive colorings to attract mates. Why primates evolved to use visual cues is unclear, but one reason for this is that the higher primates, the ones that are more derived and less-like the ancestral mammal from which they evolved, are mostly diurnal (active during the day). This would mean that as they adapted to a new niche, they needed to find a way to survive.

The emphasis on vision can be best seen by the location of the primate's eye in relation to their head. Their eyes are towards the front of the head rather than the side. This forward rotation of the eyes allows primates to have more depth perception than other mammals and can be seen in the skulls of various primates.

Seeing depth is the result of having two *different* fields of vision that overlap, which allows the brain to complete a three-dimensional, stereoscopic, vision. To understand how your brain does this, hold your finger close to your face and alternate opening each eye. Then move your finger further away and do the same thing. You should notice that when something is closer to your eyes, there is a larger difference between what your right eye sees and what your left eye sees. This parallax allows your brain to interpret depth. This is not to say that people with only one eye cannot see depth. They can use other clues to interpret how far away different objects are. But parallax gives primates a better understanding of where the next branch is or how far away a prey item is. Another benefit of moving the eyes forward is that the pupil is at the center of the eye. This allows light to pass through the center. Primates also have relatively smaller pupils, which leads to less distortion of the image.

Many primates have also evolved the ability to see three different types of color. Birds, reptiles and many fish have four types of opsin proteins, which allows them to be tetrachromatic, seeing four different kinds of color. Most mammals, however, are dichromatic and can only distinguish blue, green, yellow, violet. This is due to ancestral mammals being nocturnal, for which seeing in color was not useful and might have been detrimental.

Seeing in color is a complex process. For most humans, this is done via the production of three different types of cones that allow us to see different types of colors: The short-wave receptors, the medium-wave receptors, and the long-wavelength receptors. These are produced via specific opsin proteins that are light sensitive. In most catarrhines (monkeys and apes the live in Africa and Asia), the genes that produce the medium and long opsins are located next to each other on the X chromosome. For platyrrhines (monkeys that live in the Americas), the medium and long opsins are produced by the same gene on the X chromosome. This means that female platyrrhines can in theory have both medium and long opsins (and thus be trichromats) while males only have one and are dichotomous.

At some point in their evolutionary history these two different groups of primates have evolved the ability to see trichromatically. It seems that the ability to distinguish between red and green was important. It could have evolved to allow them to identify red fruit among the green leaves, Or maybe it was an adaptation to distinguishing the leaves themselves, as red leaves are younger and have more nutrients.

While primates evolved a greater reliance on sight, they began to reduce their reliance on olfaction. The more primitive primates are more focused on sense of smell than the so-called higher primates (most of the monkeys and the apes) who have dry noses and smaller snouts. A rhinarium is the wet part of the nose that surrounds the nostrils. This can be seen most prominently in mammals such as dogs. Primitive primates (sometimes called the wet-nosed primates, or strepsirrhines) retain this feature, while the higher primates have lost this rhinarium.

LIFE IN THE TREES AND DIET

Another tendency seen in primates is that they are adapted to an arboreal lifestyle. While not all primates live in trees, many do. And those that do not often retain aspects of their ancestral condition. These adaptations to life in the trees are seen in much of a primate's anatomy.

Hypnic jerks, the twitching in their leg many people feel while falling asleep, may be a holdover from when our primate ancestors slept in trees and is an involuntary response as the brain thinks it is falling out of a tree.

Most primates have hands and feet that can be used to grasp objects such as a tree branch. This is because they have highly mobile digits and opposable thumbs to help them hold onto things as well as support their bodies. Some walk on their hands or knuckles, while other support themselves on their palms or fists.

Being able to grasp requires complex musculature and a thumb that can swing to oppose the other fingers. All primates with the exception of living humans have the ability to grasp with their feet due to their divergent big toe. As we will see in the next chapter, the evolution of bipedalism led to human ancestors losing this feature and evolving a derived, bipedal foot morphology (though in some sense the oddest of the primates is the orangutan in terms of how they walk, as rather than landing on the back of the foot they strike the ground with the edge of their foot first).

Primates have an enhanced tactile perception as well. This can be seen in our fingerprints. These dermal ridges probably function to help primates hold onto a branch and avoid slipping. Fingerprints also enhance the feelings in the tips of your fingers, something that is helpful if you are a primate hunting for insects or a human using a tool.

Connected to this enhanced sense of touch is the evolution of nails rather than claws in many primates. While unclear exactly why nails evolved, they protect the sensitive tips of the fingers (this sensitivity is clear if you cut your nail too close). Nails could also be used to pinch things like seeds and other food items. This feature is also reflected in the skeleton, as scholars studying primate origins can examine the tips of the digits of a fossil mammal to see if the surface reflects nails or claws.

Most humans are obligate bipeds, meaning that they can only easily walk on two legs on the ground. But as an order this is fairly unique. Some primates such as marmosets live in the trees and are arboreal while others, like baboons, are terrestrial and spend their time on the ground. Lemurs are clingers and leapers, jumping from branch to branch, while chimps are knuckle walkers. Some, like the gibbons, are brachiators, where their body is supported by alternating forelimbs on to the branches.

A wide and varied diet is another important tendency in primates. Folivores concentrate on plants, frugivores eat fruit, carnivores eat meat, insectivores feed on insects, and omnivores have a mixed diet. Because of the wide range of differences, primate teeth and jaws can be used to inform on their dietary niche.

One of the primary traits that is correlated with diet is body size. Folivory is seen in large primates like gorillas while insectivory is seen more often in smaller primates. The reason for this is that larger mammals have *relatively* lower energetic requirements. Basal metabolic rate (the amount of energy needed while resting) gets smaller *relative to body mass* as animals get bigger. In other words, a large animal must eat more food in absolute terms but relative to its body size it does not have to take in as much energy rich food. That might seem counterintuitive but reflects how body mass scales relative to energy needed per unit of time. This fact, called Kleiber's law, explains a lot of variation we see in dietary niches.

Applying this to primates allows us to understand much about primate diet and adaptations. Imagine you are a primatologist and spend time watching both a 20 kg (44 lb) proboscis monkey and a 0.1 kg (approx. 3 oz) tarsier. In one day of foraging, they both might encounter 35 insects. For the small tarsier, this may meet the protein needs (both relative and absolute), but 35 insects is not sufficient for 20 kg monkey species (either relative or absolute). At the same time, the proboscis would be able to feed on leaves that would take the smaller primate too long to digest. This suggest that the upper size limit of insectivory is based on availability, while the lower limit of folivory is imposed by metabolic parameters. Some primates seem to have found ways around this outcome of Kleiber's law. The chimps that Goodall observed eating termites used the grass to obtain a lot of insects at once by termite fishing.

Primates' diverse diet is also reflected in their teeth. While you might not have spent much time thinking about them, anthropologists spend a lot of time wondering about teeth. Their main function is to help you cut, grind, and tear food into smaller pieces (something that most of us only realize this we can no longer use our teeth for those functions). By looking at dental variation we can not only learn about extant primate adaptations but also apply these ideas to fossil primates. For example, if we find primates today with specialized incisor teeth for certain behaviors, and then find a similar adaptation in an extinct primate, that could give us an indication of the diet and behavior of that extinct primate species.

Primates have retained the four major mammalian teeth types: **incisors**, which help to cut into food; **canines**, which help to tear food; **premolars/bicuspids** and **molars**, which help us chew, crush, and grind food. The variation we see in primate teeth comes from the shape of these teeth and the exact number of teeth they have.

We use what is called a **dental formula** to keep track of the number of teeth on in the upper and lower jaw. Since primates are symmetrical, the formula just counts one side of the jaw. A dental formula is created by counting the teeth in one half of the upper and lower jaw, giving a count in the number of incisors, canines, premolars and molars in the upper and lower quadrants. For most adult humans, the dental formula is 2123/2123, which means there are 2 canines, 1 incisor, 2 premolars and 3 molars in each quadrant of the upper and lower jaw, for a total of 32 teeth. Of course, this number is highly variable in humans. You might have had your third molars (sometimes called wisdom teeth) removed due to overcrowding (see Chapter 6 for why this overcrowding occurred).

The ancestral mammals that primates evolved from had a dental formula of 3143/3143 (so 3 incisors, 1 canine, 4 premolars and 3 molars. The ancestral primate had a dental formula of 2143/2143. Catarrhines, such as humans, have 2123/2123.

Besides the number and type of teeth, the actual morphology of a tooth can also tell us a lot. The surface of the molars and pre-molars helps the primate to crush and grind its food. For a primate that eats insects, having a molar that has pointed cusps helps it to crush an insect. Having more of a crest on the molar surface is more common for those that need to break apart leaves, as seen in gorillas.

Some teeth are even more specialized. Many lemurs have evolved to have their lower canines look more incisor-like. In doing so they have their front six teeth on their mandible form what is called a tooth comb, which forms a scraper-like device that allows them to groom their fur and scrape gum from trees. The incisors are long, slender, and project forward while the canines take on a more incisor-like shape.

SOCIAL LIFE

The social life of primates has received a lot of attention. Most primates travel, eat, and sleep in groups. In this sense, living in a group can be seen as an adaptation. Living in groups is not always easy and can be the source of much conflict, but it also has a lot of benefits for a species.

The ways in which primates interact with each other is com-plex and often differs based on the animals biological sex. Pair bonds, enduring relationships between two adults, are common. Monogamy is a system where mating occurs between one male and one female. This is fairly rare in mammals, but humans are sometimes described as monogamous. For some, it simply means when reproduction is predominantly between one male and one female. While this might not fit the colloquial idea of monogamy, it seems accurate that we form long term pair bonds with mates, something that does not seem to occur in chimpanzees and many other primates. The fact that humans pair bond with their mates, then, presents us with an evolutionary puzzle. But as we will see in the next chapter there is a lot of uncertainty about the behavior of our early ancestors.

Compared to most mammals, primates have fewer babies and space them out more. This gives the mom more time to invest in each child. **Kinship** looks at the degree of genetic relationship between individuals. An individual may receive a selective benefit by helping kin. This process, called kin selection, could explain some of what we see in primate behavior.

The psychologist Harry Harlow (1905–1981) was interested in the question of the role of a mother's love in raising a child. At the time, many psychologists argued that human babies would be 'spoiled' if their parents picked them up when they cried. Harlow designed a series of experiments that to our eyes today (and probably at the time) seem horrific. He separated a baby rhesus monkey from its mom and gave the baby a choice of two surrogate 'mothers' made of wire. One of these had a bottle of food attached to it but nothing else. The other was cloth-covered. Harlow suggested that if all an infant needs is nourishment, they would prefer the wire 'mother' since that one had the food.

But Harlow showed that the babies preferred the cloth mother. He suggested this meant that the contact and close comfort that the babies felt from the cloth mother was important. Again, this kind of study is now seen as cruel. But Harlow's point was to show that love and comfort does matter. Later scholars have tried to study the effects of separation in more ethical ways, but all these studies have critics who suggest they are inhumane.

We also see a lot of variation in childcare. For example, while a female owl monkey is the one who nurses the baby, she will often make the father be the one who carried the kid (males carry them roughly 90% of the time).

Communication is the intentional transfer of information between individuals. For most primates, living in groups requires them to communicate with each other. Vervet monkeys have different calls to alert the group of the presence of different predators. These calls are acoustically distinct and elicit appropriate responses in their group members (for example, the eagle call makes them look up and the snake call makes them look down). Research suggests that as they age, vervets get better at classifying predators. See below for more on this system.

The study of self-medication by non-human animals is known as zoopharmacognosy. It is difficult to know for certain why an animal eats certain things, but primatologists and animal behavior experts have recorded many examples of nonhuman animals using dirt, grass, and other materials as aids to feeling better when sick. These behaviors can also include ingesting materials they normally do not eat (such as leaf- and seed-swallowing) and using a topical material. Tamarins, for example, sometimes rub their bodies against specific trees whose sap have antibiotic properties. Chimpanzees in Tanzania will fold whole leaves and swallow them, perhaps to help remove parasitic worms. And lemurs are known to rub millipedes on their fur.

Some have argued that studying primate self-medication can help humans find new drugs and compounds. It also clues us into the evolutionary origins of medicine. The field of evolutionary medicine uses these and other studies to help treat and understand diseases. Applying an evolutionary approach to the study of disease allows doctors and researchers to better understand why we get sick and how to treat illnesses. Antibacterial resistance, during which bacteria evolve resistance to antibiotics, is a result of mutations and natural selection. This can explain how drug-resistant strains of various diseases can spread quickly.

CLADISTICS

One of the most confusing aspects of primates is how to organize them. Since there are more than 500 species in the primate order we need to put them into meaningful groups.

Earlier scholars used a division between **prosimians** and **anthropoids**. Prosimians are the more primitive primates, such as the lemurs, lorises, and tarsiers. They have wet noses and scent glands, and many of them are nocturnal. Anthropoids are more derived in their overall morphology, having traits that are more removed from the normal mammal pattern, such as larger brains relative to body size, a fused mandible, and larger body size. With at least one exception, the anthropoids are diurnal.

However, this division of prosimians and anthropoids is problematic because it creates groups that are not **monophyletic**. When classifying animals in an evolutionary sense, groups should consist of an ancestor and *all* of its descendants. When the prosimian category was created less was known about primate cladistics. We now know that prosimians are a **paraphyletic** group because it includes the tarsiers, which are closer to the anthropoids than to the members of the prosimian group. There are some behavioral similarities within the prosimians and some scholars do use the prosimian nomenclature to stress these similarities, but the terms prosimian and anthropoid are not used for taxonomic work.

Today, the major divisions for primates is at the Suborder where we distinguish between the **strepsirrhines** and **haplorhines**. Figure 4.1 shows one possible primate taxonomy, though the specific groupings of many primates, especially extinct ones, is often debated.

The strepsirrhines have noses that are wet while haplorhines have dry noses (since you are a haplorhine you too have a dry nose!). Strepsirrhines have retained long noses as well, with small bones in the inner nose to aid in olfaction. Most strepsirrhines are arboreal and have smaller brains compared to the haplorhines.

The more derived haplorhines have evolved toward a more vision-based sensory system, which can be seen in the bones of their skulls. Strepsirrhines have a postorbital bar, a bony ring that surrounds the eye, while the haplorhines have a postorbital plate or closure, a wall of bone behind the eye. While most of their digits have nails, strepsirrhines retain a claw on their second toe that they use for grooming.

Strepsirrhines thus have more primitive traits than the haplorhines. This group, which includes lemurs, galagos, and lorises are sometimes referred to lower primates since they are less derived than the haplorhines. But this does not mean that they are not relevant for studying bioanthropology. Lemurs, for example, are very social and have adapted to a wide range of environments within the island of Madagascar. While now extinct, there were even giant lemurs that were close to a gorilla in size.

The living haplorhines are further divided into two categories at the parvorder: the **platyrrhines** and **catarrhines.** Platyrrhines

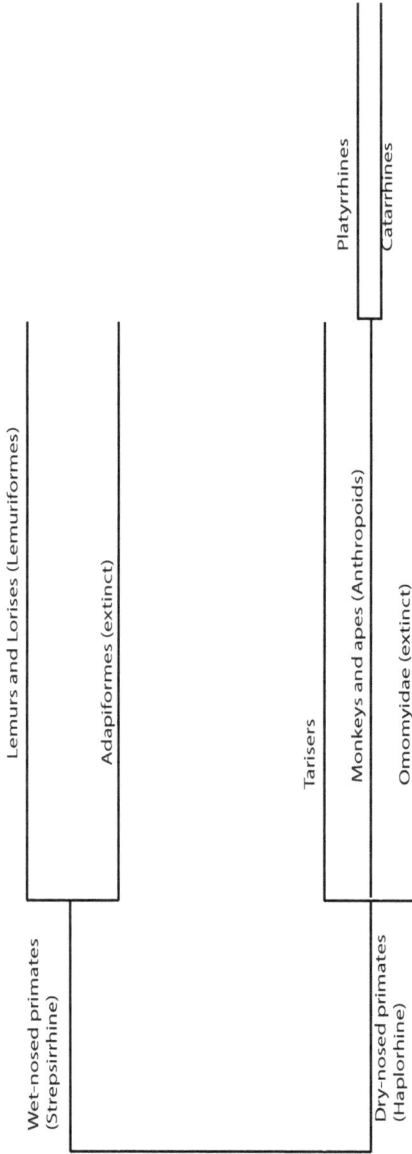

Figure 4.1 A plausible primate taxonomy.

TABLE 4.2 Comparison of some of the main differences between strepsirrhines and haplorhines.

Strepsirrhines	Haplorhines
Wet-noses that are long	Dry-noses that are short
Smaller braincase	Larger braincase
More emphasis on sense of smell	More emphasis on sense of vision
Mostly nocturnal and arboreal	Mostly diurnal
Lemurs, lorises	Tarsiers, platyrrhines, catarrhines

have outward facing nostrils and are found in the Americas.
Catarrhines, meanwhile, are found in Africa and Asia and have
downward facing nostrils (the names hint at these differences:
platyrrhine means 'broad nosed' while catarrhine means 'down-
nosed'). Sometimes these two groups are called New World and
Old World Primates, but scholars today avoid these terms due to
their colonial implications.

Another difference is the number of teeth they have. Catarrhines
have a 2123/2123 dental formula while most platyrrhines have
2133/2133, meaning they have four extra teeth. Platyrrhines often
have prehensile tails which they can use to hold onto things, while
no Catarrhine has that ability.

As an example, we know that humans are primates with the
dental formula 2123/2123 and we have downward-facing nostrils.
This tells us that *Homo sapiens* are haplorhines and are in the catarrhine parvorder.

The platyrrhines are organized into five families, though the
exact placement and arrangement changes as we learn more about
their evolutionary history. These include the sakis and uakaris,
howler, spider, and muriquis; capuchin and squirrel monkeys;
marmoset and tamarins; and owl (night) monkeys. As an example of the complexity of these primates the callitrichids (marmosets and tamarins) are sometimes referred to as phylogenetic
dwarves, since they are much smaller than other platyrrhines. It
is not known why they are so small, but some have argued that
their habitat of the Amazon rainforest has led them to adapt to the
patchwork landscape in a sort of island dwarfism. They are also
known for having twins more often than any other primate. And,

unlike the pattern seen in most primates, male callitrichids invest a lot of energy in caring for the young.

The catarrhines (monkeys and apes of Africa and Asia) can be further divided into two main groups: the **cercopithecoids** (monkeys) and the **hominoids** (apes). The monkeys are then divided into two subfamilies—**Cercopithecinae** and **Colobinae**—with cercopithecines being typically the larger of the two cercopithecoids groups. They have cheek pouches (pockets between the teeth and the cheek where they can store food) and ischial callosities (sitting pads that let them sleep upright without falling off a branch). Cercopithecines include baboons, vervet monkeys, and macaques. The patas monkey, which can run at up to 35 mph, and the mandrill, the world's largest monkey, are also in this group.

The Colobinae are mostly arboreal. They have sacculated stomachs for foregut fermentation and no cheek pouches. Most of their diet comes from leaves, and they have specialized teeth that allow them to sheer leaves into smaller pieces and their salivary glands are adapted to help break down leaves. Interestingly, they cannot fully breakdown leaves and need to rely on bacteria in their bodies, which means it takes them a long time to fully digest their food. This group includes colobus, langur, and proboscis monkeys. Proboscis monkeys are also known as long-nosed monkeys, as they have oddly big noses, with male proboscis monkey's noses being so large that they can hang below their mouths. These noses seem to function as both an auditory and visual signal to female proboscis monkeys. Visually, large noses signal both quality and social status, while loud nasalized calls, in a forest with low visibility, serves as an acoustic signal.

The hominoids, colloquially called the apes, are the group of primates that humans belong to. A quick way to tell the difference between a monkey and an ape is that apes do not have tails while monkeys do. Hominoids also have larger brains. Dentally they have specific patterns to their molar teeth which allow paleontologists to identify apes in the fossil record, a useful trait for those interested in hominoid evolution. Apes also have much more flexibility in their shoulder joints, a trait that evolved alongside evolving larger bodies. Being able to rotate shoulders and extend elbows allowed hominoids to carefully climb down trees.

The apes are divided into the large bodied and the smaller bodied species. The large-body apes are the gorillas, orangutans, chimpanzees, and humans. The smaller ones are sometimes called lesser apes due to their physical size, but primatologists who study gibbons prefer the term *wee apes* to make it clear that they are not less valued, just smaller.

The gibbons, aka the wee apes, spend most of their time in trees. They have very long arms and very flexible wrists, allowing them to **brachiate,** swinging from branches. They 'sing' to let others know of their presence and some mated pairs of gibbons sing duets to form bonds. The siamang is one of the largest gibbons. Found in Sumatra, they weight up to 14 kg (approx. 31 lb) and have a large throat sac that lets them produce a loud sound. On the ground they are bipedal and look somewhat ridiculous because they must keep their long arms up in the air as they walk

Orangutans have marked sexual dimorphism, with the males being as much as twice the weight of females. Mostly frugivorous, they have what has been called 'mental maps,' which allow them to know where and when fruit is masting. As the most arboreal of the large apes, they spend most of their time in the trees using their long arms and shorter legs to scramble amongst the trees, grasping branches with all four limbs in a manner called low quadrumanous climbing.

Gorillas are the largest living primates, with males getting up to 220 kg (approx. 485 lb). As mentioned above, they are folivorous, with most of their diet coming from leaves. The silverback, the male gorilla who is the 'leader' of his group, is responsible for protection against rogue males & predators and has a harem of adult females with exclusive mating access (though this exclusivity might be an illusion).

When a silverback loses control of his harem through death or old age, the new silverback will often commit **infanticide**, killing the young gorillas. This occurs because the new silverback is not related to the current young. Females will not go into estrus while a baby is young, and the new silverback must wait till the infant is weaned. But if the babies are killed, a mother will become receptive to mating with the new silverback. Infanticide has been reported in many primates, and probably occurs for similar reasons.

Chimpanzees are our closest relatives and are split into two species: the common chimpanzees and the bonobo. Common chimps are some of the best studied apes in the world and much is known about their biology, behavior, and culture (it would take a whole book to cover everything that is known about them!). As omnivores their diets are very varied. Much has been made of their hunting abilities, with some chimps being very adept at hunting colobus monkeys. Western chimpanzees in Senegal have been reported to use spears, taking limbs off trees and sharpening one end. They then stick the sharpened end into spaces where galagos (a strepsirrhine primates) sleep to hunt them.

The social behavior of common chimps shows that a core group of usually related males tend to be in charge and there is a high frequency of agonistic, violent behavior. They are polygamous and promiscuous, with females dispersing from their natal group.

Bonobos, sometimes called pygmy chimpanzees because they are more gracile, are less well-known. Perhaps the most celebrated aspect of the bonobos is how their social system differs from common chimpanzees. Unlike the common chimpanzees, bonobos have a matriarchal system with females in charge. There is very low frequency of agonistic behavior and social stress is ameliorated by non-procreative sexual behavior. Both sexes engage in same sex pairings, with female bonobos engaged in mutual genital rubbing behavior more often, perhaps to bond socially with each other. Infanticide is also much less common than in chimpanzees. It is thought that they use sex to lower aggression.

LANGUAGE

The question of whether a nonhuman primate could learn language has been at the center of much debate and controversy. While today few scholars are trying to teach apes to communicate via sign language, for a long time such work was at the forefront of psychological research. It is hard to say for sure what the results of these studies are, but while it seems like apes have the capacity for some aspects of language, such as being able to learn and categorize objects, they do not have what is known as shared intentionality.

Vervet monkeys have a series of complex alarm calls, giving distinct calls for different predators such as eagles, snakes, and leopards. These calls elicit different responses in other vervets. When they hear the eagle call from another vervet, the monkeys will search the sky and then often hide in the bushes, while for a snake call they will search the ground. Some primatologists argue that since the calls they give for eagle or snake are arbitrary in their specific sound, this would make is a symbolic sign. While discussed more in Chapter 6 being able to make links that are arbitrary between a sign and the thing it stands for might be the basis of human language. But as vervets are not hominoids, other anthropologists have suggested that this adaptation does not inform on human language.

The question that the ape language projects tried to answer is to what extent does human language differ from communication seen in nonhuman primates. But this requires us to know what sets human language apart from other forms of communication, and that has not been an easy question to answer. As we saw with the vervet monkeys, primates are good at communication. Animal communication is complex and often distinctive. For example, electric eels use electricity to communicate to others in ways that humans cannot (well, at least not without external tools).

In order to understand this debate, we need to know what makes human language different from other forms of communication. Language consists of syntax (the words that we use) and grammar (the rules used to put the words together). We can combine these words and rules into complex sentences to communicate ideas and thoughts in novel ways.

The question many tried to answer is if apes such as chimpanzees could learn language via social learning by living among humans. Studies in the 1970s seemed to show that apes could use sign language to communicate, but other scholars suggested that this was simply apes learning how to get the response they wanted (mostly food) and that they were not making sentences in the way humans do. Critics suggested that the apes were following unintentional cues that the human experimenter was giving.

This work generated a lot of discussion and debate, leading eventually to one of the most famous examples of ape language studies. Sue Savage-Rumbaugh and colleagues attempted to teach a bonobo (Matata) to use lexigrams, graphical symbols representing a word, to communicate. While Matata was not able to learn this, her son Kanzi (who watched his mom while the experiment was ongoing) learned to use the lexigrams. As with the way humans use language, Kanzi was not being directly taught but rather learned via interactions with others. This was relevant since Kanzi's reward was not food but communication itself.

Kanzi was very smart and seems to understand that word order matters when his humans asked him to do things (i.e., 'put A on B' means A goes on top of B). So, there is some knowledge of grammar but he did not seem to do the opposite (i.e., does not produce and ask for things in the same way). The team working with Kanzi showed that most (96%) of Kanzi's communications were asking for things. Indeed, critics have argued that apes like Kanzi only sign to request the things and objects they want. This leads some to ask if this is communication in the way humans do it (influence what others think) or just for him to get what he wanted. In other words, are apes only using imperative purposes rather than declarative ones. But others suggest that this is too simplistic and ignores work that shows that some of these apes have a much more complex language system.

Michael Tomasello has studied this question in depth and suggests that the ape language projects have shown that they can learn to get what they want by using communication to direct the attention of others. But he suggests that they do not seem to naturally use communication for other social reasons such as letting others known about events. They also do not seem to understand what a communication partner may or may not know.

For a unique look at some of the internal debates of early ape language projects see the film *Project Nim*. Such studies require a lot of funding, and apes are long-lived animals who, in such studies, are often not able to be integrated into a more natural habitat once a study is over. Ethically and practically, it seems that such studies will not be done anytime soon.

WHY IS PRIMATOLOGY PART OF ANTHROPOLOGY?

If bioanthropology is about understanding humans' place in nature, what role do non-human primates play in this science? The primatologist Phyllis Dolhinow argues that 'It is obvious that there must be an interactive association between anthropology and primatology if we are to sustain the nonhuman primates. This cooperation requires an accurate and complete understanding both of the requirements of the nonhuman primates and of the human cultures that threaten the damage.'

The Primates order encompasses a lot of variation, but there are some 'tendencies' that lump them all together. Humans are primates and thus we share a lot with the rest of the non-human primates. But, we are also highly derived. The **comparative technique** asks if a trait is unique or distinctive to humans or if it is shared with other non-human primates. Using the comparative technique, primatologists can understand the evolutionary forces that helped to create those behaviors or adaptations. In one sense, the lesson of twentieth-century primatology was that there are not many behaviors and traits that only humans have.

In order to study primates, anthropologists can do fieldwork in their range country, observing them in their native habitat. Others work with captive primates in zoos. Both captive and field studies are used to understand the complex nature of primate behavior and cognition and there are pros and cons to both approaches. Field work might give a better understanding of how the animal lives in the 'wild' but it is not cheap. Moreover, a researcher's presence in the field could, in theory, influence the primates themselves. Captive studies are easier to run and scientists can 'control' some of the environment if they want to study specific aspects. It is also often easier to obtain biomedical samples from captive primates. Controversially, they have been used in biomedical research and psychological studies. Examining how baboons respond to stress suggests how stress affects humans.

Since many primate species live in large social groups, they also can help anthropologists understand the evolution of group dynamics. Living with a group of others is not easy. Nonhuman primates do not have language the way humans do, so they need to find other ways to communicate and deal with the stresses of living with others. Living in groups gives defense from predators and other groups, as well as access to mating and resources. But group life inevitably leads to conflict (both within groups and between groups). The skills and traits that humans have, such as language, may have been adaptations to dealing with the problems of living among many others.

Studying primates also lets us understand ecological adaptations. Primatology asks what makes this Order so accomplished at living in such a wide variety of ecological zones. For example, the aye-aye is a strepsirrhine that lives on the island of Madagascar. They have evolved unique middle fingers that are long and narrow, which they use to hunt via percussive foraging, tapping on trees to locate grubs in the trees. They then use their teeth to open a hole in the tree and use their finger to grab the grub from the tree (a study from 2022 discovered that they also use their long, slender fingers to pick their nose …). Such adaptations point to the role of natural selection in human evolution.

Primate behavior clues us into the ways in which our early ancestors lived and behaved and can provide models for where humans come from. Both baboons and chimpanzees have been used as models of what life was like for our early ancestors, since both have traits that suggest they could be exemplars of early human behavior in the deep past. But other monkeys and apes can also inform on why and how human ancestors evolved certain traits.

All of this can then be used when studying our early human ancestors. Seeing how primate behaviors are recorded in the skeletal system lets anthropologists make informed hypotheses about the behavior of extinct species. For example, male apes such as chimpanzees often have large canines as a signal to other males that they should be wary of their strength. This is a reflection of their mating system where males mate with multiple females. If we find human ancestors that do not have large canines that might imply that their social system is different than that of other apes.

Primatology is part of bioanthropology, then, because it gives us unique insights into the biology and behavior of the order of mammals that humans belong to. Primates are also culturally important. Primates have roles in many societies and are parts of many creation myths and stores. The field of ethnoprimatology studies how humans and nonhuman primates interact with each other.

CHAPTER SUMMARY

Anthropologists often have debated the use of the word 'culture' in nonhuman animals. If we think of culture as behavior that is shared, learned, and socially transmitted then perhaps it is common outside of humans. Non-human culture has been argued for chimps, bonobos, orangutans, capuchins, spider monkeys, meerkats, dolphins, whales, birds, and some fish among others.

The primate order consists of around 500 species. Since humans are primates, studying the evolution, adaptations, and behaviors of the nonhuman primates is critical for our understanding of what makes us human. Using the comparative approach, we can learn what is distinctive about humans with respect to other primates. As we have seen, it is hard today for sure what behaviors are unique to humans. nonhuman primates seem to have culture (at least based on some definitions) and some monkeys and apes even use tools.

Primatologists today are also careful not to privilege certain species. While it is true that chimpanzees are our closest living relatives, this does not mean that we should only look to the apes. Primates far removed from human evolution can tell us a lot about the evolution of life history, parenting, diet, and learning to live in a group. The next chapters take all we have learned about primatology and apply it to the fossil record, asking how we can go from bones to behavior.

1. Primatology is part of bioanthropology. Primatologists study the taxonomy, behavior, and biology of the nonhuman primates and these data can help us understand human evolution.
2. Primates are highly varied in the adaptations but there are certain tendencies such as arboreal lifestyle, high parental investment, and a varied diet that are seen in many of them.
3. Primate taxonomy is very complex and often changing, but the general classifications separate the higher primates from the more primitive ones. Among the higher primates we see adaptations to relying more on vision than on olfaction.
4. Social life is a very important aspect for most primates. Learning how to live in a group is not easy and primates solve these problems in different ways.

FURTHER READING

Bezanson, Michelle, and Allison McNamara. 2019. The What and Where of Primate Field Research May Be Failing Primate Conservation. *Evolutionary Anthropology* 28(4): 166–178. https://doi.org/10.1002/evan .21790. *A review that looks at some of the issues of contemporary primatology, especially looking at the issues that while there are over 500 species fewer than half of these are represented in much the primate literature.*

Cheney, Dorothy L., and Robert M. Seyfarth. 2008. *Baboon Metaphysics: The Evolution of a Social Mind.* University of Chicago Press. *A view from two prominent scholars about what baboons know and how they form relationships and friendships.*

de Waal, Frans B. M. 2006. Bonobo Sex and Society. *Scientific American*, June 1. www.scientificamerican.com/article/bonobo-sex-and-society-2006 -06. *One of the leading experts in bonobos describing their lifeways.*

Gebo, Daniel. 2014. *Primate Comparative Anatomy.* Johns Hopkins University Press. *A great resource comparing primate anatomy with wonderful illustrations.*

Kaisin, Olivier, Fernanda Corrêa Rocha, Rodrigo Gonçalves Amaral, Felipe Bufalo, Gabriel Pavan Sabino, and Laurence Culot. 2022. A Universal Pharmacy: Possible Self-Medication Using Tree Balsam by Multiple Atlantic Forest Mammals. *Biotropica* 54(3): 576–582. https://doi.org/10 .1111/btp.13095. *Example of primates using self-medication.*

Pruetz, Jill D, and Paco Bertolani. 2007. Savanna Chimpanzees, Pan Troglodytes Verus, Hunt with Tools. *Current Biology* 17(5): 412–417. https://doi.org/10.1016/j.cub.2006.12.042. *Description of chimps using spear tools to hunt.*

Regan, B. C., C. Julliot, B. Simmen, F. Viénot, P. Charles-Dominique, and J. D. Mollon. 2001. Fruits, Foliage and the Evolution of Primate Colour Vision. *Philosophical Transactions of the Royal Society of London B* 356(1407): 229–283. https://doi.org/10.1098/rstb.2000.0773. *Good overview of what we know about primate color vision.*

Scott, Jeremiah E. 2019. Macroevolutionary Effects on Primate Trophic Evolution and Their Implications for Reconstructing Primate Origins. *Journal of Human Evolution* 133 (August):1–12. https://doi.org/10.1016/j .jhevol.2019.05.001. *Nice overview of primate evolution.*

Tomasello, Michael. 2017. What Did We Learn from the Ape Language Studies? In *Bonobos: Unique in Mind, Brain, and Behavior*, edited by Brian Hare and Shinya Yamamoto. Oxford University Press. *An overview of some of the work done on trying to teach apes to communicate via human language.*

5

PALEOANTHROPOLOGY (I)
Early Hominins

CHAPTER OVERVIEW

Paleoanthropologists specialize in human evolution. In this sub-field, the question of what makes humans distinctive is examined via fossils, genetics, and the archeological record. Earlier anthropologists thought the answer to this question would have to do with the use of tools, but we know now that many other species use tools, including many nonhuman primates, cetaceans (dolphins and whales), many birds, and even some fish and invertebrates. Other behaviors, such as language use, cooking, consciousness, big game hunting, and complex tool use may be uniquely human but when they originated is uncertain. Knowing when and why these evolved is the purview of paleoanthropology.

This chapter seeks to understand how we became human, focusing on the early aspects of human origins, from when human and chimp ancestors split up to the evolution of *Homo sapiens*. It starts with what we might expect an early member of our clade (called the hominins) looks like and then discusses the fossil and archaeological record. We then look at some of the different hominin species. The chapter ends with a discussion of major debates in early human origins. The next chapter looks at how humans spread across the globe and what happened when they met other hominin populations. And as we will see, we can trace the origins of contemporary humans through fossils, archaeology, primatology, genetics and human biology (not coincidentally we have looked at many of these fields already!).

DOI: 10.4324/9781003390442-6

WHAT IS A HOMININ?

A hominin is a primate more closely related to humans than to any other living primate. In other words, they are evolutionarily closer to us than they are to the chimpanzees and bonobos. Figure 5.1 shows the relationship between hominins and other apes.

Today the only living hominin is us: *Homo sapiens*. But in the past, there were many different species of hominin, some of which were contemporaneous with each other. How these hominins interacted when they met each other is unclear. We do know, however, that some interbreeding occurred since we see signals of gene flow between hominins. The most famous example of this are the Neandertals, a population of hominins that lived in Europe and Asia during the last ice age (classic Neandertals date to 130,000–30,000 years ago).

Table 5.1 lists just some of the potential hominins. It is important to remember that each of these species is a hypothesis; a proposal

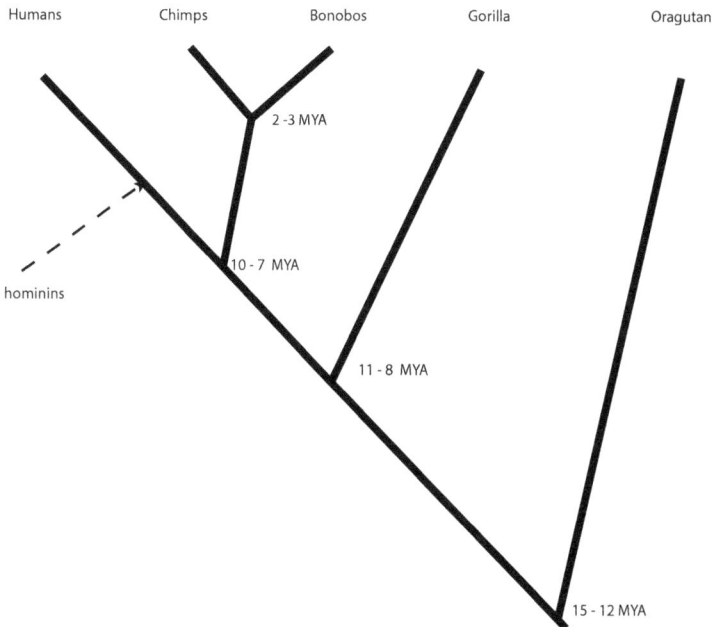

Figure 5.1 Relationship between hominins and other apes.

TABLE 5.1 Some of the proposed hominin species. mya = million years ago; kya = thousand years ago.

Species name	First appearance	Last appearance	Locations found	Notes
Sahelanthropus tchadensis	~7 mya	~7 mya	Chad	Oldest proposed hominin, known mostly from its cranium
Orrorin tugenensis	~6 mya	~5.7 mya	Kenya	Best known of the early, pre-australopithecus hominins
Ardipithecus ramidus	4.8 mya	4.4 mya	Ethiopia	
Australopithecus anamensis	4.2 mya	3.8 mya	Kenya	Earliest known australopithecus
Australopithecus afarensis	3.9 mya	3 mya	Ethiopia and Tanzania	Best known from the Dinkinesh /Lucy fossil
Australopithecus africanus	3.7 mya	2.6/2.3 mya		Taung fossil was first hominin found in Africa
Australopithecus bahrelghazali	3.5 mya	3.5 mya	Chad	Only one fragment of mandible has been found
Australopithecus garhi	2.5 mya	2.5 mya	Ethiopia	Known from one skull found in Bouri, Ethiopia. Found in association with cut marked bones
Australopithecus / Paranthropus boisei	2.5 mya	1.31 mya	Eastern Africa	May have used stone tools; coexisted alongside members of the genus *Homo*
Australopithecus / Paranthropus robustus	2.27 mya	0.96 mya	Southern Africa	Some data to suggest that used bone tools
Homo habilis	2.8 mya	1.5 mya	Eastern and Southern Africa	Best associated with Olodwan toolkit

(Continued)

TABLE 5.1 (Continued)

Species name	First appearance	Last appearance	Locations found	Notes
Australopithecus sediba	1.9 mya	1.9 mya	South Africa	Found at one site in Malapa, South Africa represented by two skeletons
Homo rudolfensis	1.9 mya	1.8 mya	Kenya and Tanzania	Some scholars lump these fossils into *H. habilis* while others think its larger brain and teeth make it a separate species
Homo floresiensis	100 kya	~50 kya	Indonesia	Their small size may be result of island dwarfism
Neandertals	250 kya	40 kya	Europe, SW Asia	Some suggest these belong in the species *H. sapiens* while others prefer the designation *Homo neanderthalensis*
Denisovans	250 kya?	30 kya?	Asia	Mostly known from genetics and a few fossils
Homo naledi	335 kya	235 kya	Rising Star Cave, South Africa	Small cranial capacity and a mosaic of primitive and derived traits
Homo sapiens	300 kya	—	Global	Only extant hominin
Homo antecessor	1.2 mya	800 kya	Europe	Some primitive and derived traits. Could be the ancestor of humans and neandertals
Homo erectus	1.9 mya	110 kya	Africa, Asia	Associated with Acheulean stone tools; may be first hominin to control fire. Some separate into two species, *H. erectus* and *H. ergaster*

(Continued)

TABLE 5.1 (Continued)

Species name	First appearance	Last appearance	Locations found	Notes
Homo heidelbergensis	1.3 mya (?)	200 kya	Asia, Africa, Europe	Could be the ancestor of humans and neandertals, but some recent work requires rethinking this
Homo longi	146 kya	—	Asia	Known mostly from the Harbin skull. New work suggests this skull may be Denisovan

to explain the types of variation found in the fossil record. Some of these proposed species are more controversial than others.

To understand where our species came from, we can compare contemporary humans to the nonhuman primates we studied in the last chapter. One obvious difference is how we locomote. Humans are obligate bipeds, meaning that many of us walk on two legs. Because this is a clear difference between humans and the other apes, the origin of bipedalism is one of the major questions in human evolution. Surprisingly enough, there is no clear explanation for exactly why hominins evolved to be fully bipedal.

Other traits that may represent significant changes between us and other living primates are a reduction in sexual dimorphism, the ability to make complex tools, and our unique social behaviors. We also have developed a **theory of mind**, which allows humans to understand that other people have mental states such as beliefs and desires and emotions. This theory of mind could be at the core of another trait that seems distinctive to modern humans: language.

Anthropologists have studied extant primates to develop a working hypothesis for the specific skeletal traits we would expect a hominin to have. Of course, many of the behaviors and features that are distinctive of our clade do not fossilize. There is no direct way to tell if a hominin had a theory of mind, nor can we easily ascertain from a fossil if the species had language. Because of this, we concentrate on evidence of bipedalism and the degree of sexual dimorphism, behaviors that have direct impacts on a species functional anatomy.

Humans are normally so good at walking that we rarely think about how difficult it really is. Every time we walk, we are essentially falling forward and then catching ourselves. As hominins began to walk bipedally their bodies needed to adapt to this new gait. Today our hips, legs, midsection, and head all show adaptations to this unique form of locomotion. These anatomical features are the result of millions of years of evolution that have made humans efficient bipeds. The first bipeds, however, were not as efficient as we are today. They retained adaptations to life in the trees, perhaps a reflection of their use of arboreal sleeping spaces.

If you look at the base of the human skull you will find a large hole at the bottom where the spinal column attaches to the brain (anatomists call this feature the *foramen magnum*, which is Latin for big hole). In humans this opening is closer to the front of the skull, allowing our spinal column to enter perpendicular to our jaw and to the ground. In a quadruped, the spinal column is parallel to the ground so the hole is more towards the back of the skull. This difference in the orientation of the foramen magnum is one of the main features paleoanthropologists look for in a fossil cranium. In fact, it was the placement of foramen magnum that first convinced scholars that the earliest hominins were found in Africa, with the discovery of the Taung Baby cranium in South Africa. This child's brain was chimp-like but its foramen magnum had a human-like orientation.

The pelvis is the feature that has the most salient information about how we walk, having evolved to help propel us forward and provide stability as we walk. It helps to picture the pelvis as a sort of ring that has two wings coming off it, with the bony parts of your hip that you can palpate being the top of those wings. Compared to chimpanzees, the human pelvis is short and broad, due to how these gluteus muscles attach. In humans, those wings flare off to the sides, giving more area for the gluteal muscles to attach to.

Changes to the femur also occurred over time. Bipedalism requires a sort of balancing act. If you watch birds walking on their two legs, they walk efficiently because their legs are close to the midline of their body. Due to our wider hips, we cannot have our legs as centered under our bodies as they are in birds. Instead, humans developed what is known as the valgus angle, where the upper leg is angled inward towards the midline of the body. If you look at another human standing up right, you might notice that their knee is closer to the middle of their body than their hips are. This is part of the adaptations to efficient bipedal walking. Toward the top of our femur, we see signs of the larger gluteal muscles. Shifting to support weight from four legs to two changed how weight gets distributed.

Other modifications happened in the human foot. Our big toe is in line with the other toes, an adaptation that helps us push off our feet as we walk. A high arch of the foot allows the foot to leverage and gives a 'spring-like' function, letting the foot propel the body forward. While members of the genus *Homo* have human-like feet, some earlier hominins retained the ability to grasp with their big toe, suggesting that early hominins were bipedal sometimes but also spent time in the trees.

While the skeletal evidence of bipedalism is clear, what is far from certain is why obligate bipedalism evolved in the first place. If bipedalism is the result of natural selection acting on the hominin phenotype, what was the fitness benefit of walking on two legs?

There are numerous hypotheses proposed for bipedalism, with some more accepted than others. Charles Darwin thought that humans became bipedal to use their hands for carrying tools and weapons. While a good hypothesis, we now know that bipedalism evolved millions of years *before* stone tools.

Several theories of bipedalism can be put into a broad category called the **savannah hypotheses**. These theories link bipedalism to adapting to living in a more open, savanna habitat with tall grasses, rather than the more forested environment that chimps currently live in. Perhaps being able to look over tall grasses for predators and to spot prey could be the prime reason for bipedal locomotion. Support for this model comes from how other primates show vigilance displays. However, recent work suggests the environment in which hominins evolved was not as savanna-like as was previously thought, so these models need rethinking.

Bipedalism may also be a feeding adaptation. This hypothesis is based on observations that chimpanzees use a bipedal gait when reaching for food on low-hanging branches. By increasing their efficiency while standing on two legs, hominins would be better able to obtain food.

Bipedal locomotion could also be the result of the need to carry objects other than tools, such as food or babies. Paleoanthropologist Owen Lovejoy has suggested that a bipedal gait evolved as a way for male hominins to provision females and children. According to this hypothesis, by providing food to their pair-bonded mates, male hominins were able to help their offspring survive and ensure that their partners were able to care for the young. This in turn let them have more children, increasing their genetic fitness. This model links together bipedalism, monogamy, and lower sexual dimorphism as all part of a new social system. Again, this is not without its critics, many of whom point out that it is a very male-biased view of human origins and does not explain the levels of sexual dimorphism seen in australopithecines.

The second aspect that paleoanthropologists look to identify hominins in the fossil record is a reduction in dentition, specifically in the size and function of the canine teeth. As we saw in Chapter 4, primates like chimpanzees and baboons often use their large canines as a signal of how powerful they are. Over hominin evolution, our canines reduced in size. This is seen in the absence of the **canine honing complex**, which is when the upper canine sharpens against the lower premolar, leaving a gap between the lower canine and lower premolar. The absence of this gap in many hominins could be a signal of reduced male–male competition, an indicator of an overall reduction in male body size.

In summary, hominins are identified in the fossil record via skeletal evidence of bipedality and changes to the dentition. These adaptations are first seen between 7 million years ago (mya) and 5 mya. It is possible that these reflect changes to the social system of early hominins. The behavioral and social system of these primates also changed. As the next section details, however, it is not always easy to find these signs in the fossil record.

GENERAL OVERVIEW OF HOMININ EVOLUTION

The sections below detail the skeletal evidence of human evolution. It is important to note that as with any science this is a rapidly changing field. New fossil discoveries and updated methodologies mean that what we know about human origins is always being adjusted. Table 5.2 provides an overview of geological time periods and human evolution.

The overall arc of human evolution begins in Africa. While the exact location is not known, sometime between 12 mya and 6 mya the last common ancestor of humans and chimpanzees was most likely spending a lot of time in the trees. How it moved and what it ate are unclear, but it was most likely very different from modern day humans and from chimpanzees.

Some set of events lead to this group splitting into two. The exact nature of speciation is unclear, but one population led to the chimps and the bonobos and the other to humans. What we

TABLE 5.2 Overview of the geological time periods in which hominins evolved.

Epoch	Geological time span	Note
Holocene	10,000 years ago to present/start of the Anthropocene	Farming and urbanization
Pleistocene	1.75 million to 10,000 years ago	Expansion of *Homo* and origin of *Homo sapiens*
Pliocene	5 million to 1.75 million years ago	*Ardipithecus/Australopithecines/* early genus *Homo*
Miocene	23 million to 5 million years ago	Earliest hominins

do know is that this last common ancestor (LCA) was probably different in its behavior and in its morphology from both humans and chimps.

The earliest fossil hominins are found in East and Central Africa. Named *Sahelanthropus tchadensis* and *Orrorin tugenensis*, these early species are fairly primitive in their morphology, with small brains and no evidence of complex culture. But they all have indications of a bipedal gait and/or a reduction in canine size. Unfortunately, the earliest hominins are known from a small set of fossils. Due to the sparse fossil record before 5 mya, not much is known about the behavior of these plausible hominins.

We know more about the genus *Ardipithecus*. While its brain was only 20% the size of *Homo sapiens*, the fossil data indicate that it was both bipedal and had small canines. Many scholars suggest it is the progenitor of later hominins. There are two proposed species of Ardipithecus, *Ardipithecus kadabba* and *Ardipithecus ramidus*, of which the latter is much better represented in the fossil record.

These earliest genera *Sahelanthropus*, *Orrorin*, and *Ardipithecus* can be collectively thought of as plausible hominins. Not all paleoanthropologists think that each of these genera are hominins. This is especially true for *Sahelanthropus* and *Orrorin* due to the fragmentary nature of these finds.

The first group of extinct primates that are accepted by all paleoanthropologists as true hominins are referred to collectively as the **australopithecines**. This group is made up of roughly 10–13

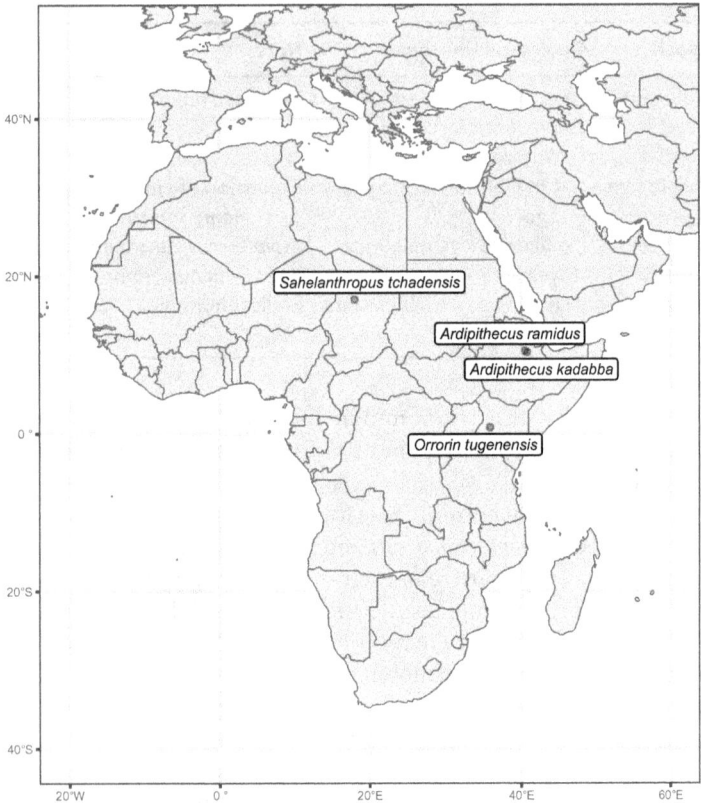

Figure 5.2 Map of sites of early hominin discoveries.

species, depending upon how one views the variation in the fossil record. The most famous of the australopithecines is Lucy, a fossil that represents the species *Australopithecus afarensis*. All australopithecines were bipedal on the ground, though many retained the ability to climb in the trees. There is reliable evidence that they used stone tools and maybe even hunted game, though this is still controversial.

At some point in the australopithecine lineage, one population split into the group that became the earliest members of our genus,

Homo. There are many proposed species of *Homo* with some of them only being discovered in the last decade.

Below is a detailed description of what we know about human origins from the earliest known hominins up to the genus *Homo.*

THE EARLY POTENTIAL HOMININS (7 MILLION TO 4 MILLION YEARS AGO)

Geneticists use the number of neutral mutations between chimpanzees and contemporary humans to estimate when the two species split, with current estimates putting this between 9 mya and 6 mya. However, because of the uncertainty in the rate of the 'molecular clock,' other studies place it closer to 12 mya.

The search for the earliest fossil hominin has produced a lot of disagreement and controversy. The earliest plausible fossil hominin yet discovered is *Sahelanthropus tchadensis.* Found in the Djurab Desert of Chad in 2001, *S. tchadensis* has a geological age of ~7 million years old. Best known from its cranium, the species has a cranial capacity of 370 cm³, around the same size of a chimpanzee's skull. Intriguingly the foramen magnum is oriented towards the front of the skull as is seen in bipeds, though the fragmentary nature of the fossil makes this hard to know for sure. *S. tchadensis* had small canines and no signs of the honing complex seen in many apes, another indicator of its potential as being part of the hominin clade.

Interestingly, limb bones discovered near the skull suggest a bipedal gait, but the overall pattern of its bones suggest a species that moved differently from modern humans. Currently not much is known about this species. It is only found at one site which makes it difficult to know much about its biology or behavior.

The other earliest plausible hominin was found in the Tugen hills in Kenya. Known as *Orrorin tugenensis,* it dates to ~5.9 mya. The species is represented mostly by limb bones and parts of the lower jaw, with a morphology suggesting that it walked bipedally. The dental remains show no sign of a honing complex. But the limited and fragmentary fossil evidence makes it difficult for anthropologists to know if it is a hominin or an ape.

The best-known potential hominin from this period is *Ardipithecus ramidus,* which dates to 4.4 mya and found in

Ethiopia. Unlike the earlier examples, *Ar. ramidus* is represented by a large number of fossils from different geological layers, representing a minimum of thirty individuals. One of the more complete skeletons is a female known as 'Ardi.' While she shows signs of bipedal locomotion, her foot retains an opposable big toe, suggesting a retention of arboreal life in the trees. As with the two previous examples, there is no sign of a honing complex in *Ardipithecus*.

The overall level of sexual dimorphism in this species is lower than seen in chimps, leading some scholars to suggest that early hominins were pair-bonding and perhaps even forming monogamous bonds. Surprisingly, Ardi lived in a forested environment, which for some is evidence against the Savannah Hypothesis described above for the origins of bipedalism.

While these three fossil species have been known for awhile we do not know how they are connected and what their relationship is to the hominins that follow. They all seem more apelike than human-like in many respects, with only their locomotion and lack of a honing complex separating them from other apes. Some of these species could have gone extinct without leaving any descendants. Most scholars would suggest that some form of *Ardipithecus ramidus* evolved into the group that became the australopithecines. It will take more fossil discoveries from this time period in order to understand how these populations interacted and connected.

THE GENUS *AUSTRALOPITHECUS* (4.2 MILLION TO 1 MILLION YEARS AGO)

The australopithecines are a diverse group of hominins. They date from between ~4.2 mya to ~1 mya, with all of them are found in the continent of Africa. They were obligate bipeds on the ground, though many retained the ability to climb and probably spent a lot of time in the trees. Overall, the group had small cranial capacities (the largest are around 600 cm^3) and have larger molars than members of the genus *Homo*. They also have jaws that project forward, making their faces less flat than is seen in *Homo sapiens*. This sticking out of the jaw and muzzle, called prognathism, becomes less extreme over human evolution.

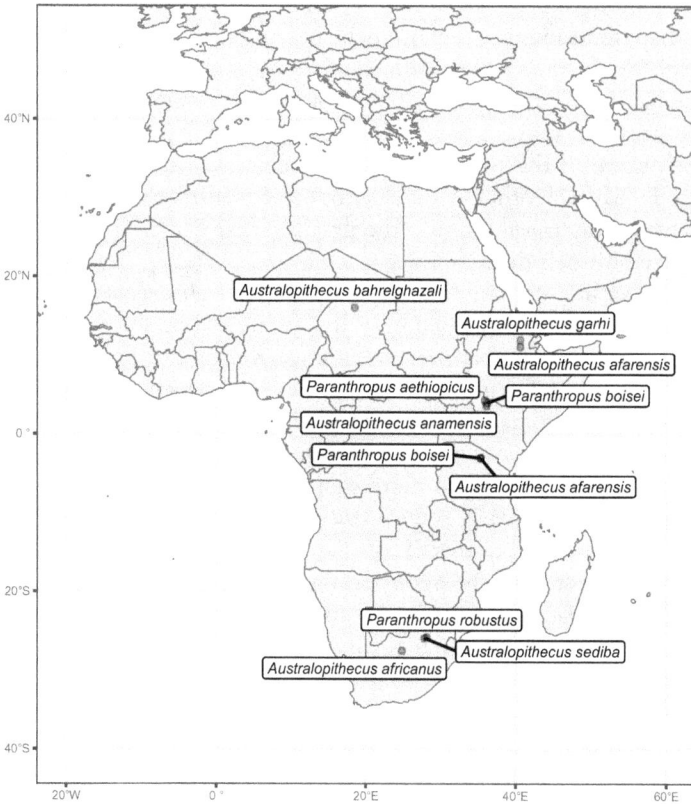

Figure 5.3 Map with location of some of the australopithecines.

The best-known species, *Australopithecus afarensis*, were probably only about 1.5 m (4.9 feet) tall and 45 kg (100 lb) in mass. While earlier scientists would often refer to australopithecines as 'bipedal apes,' recent work has shown that they may had more derived behaviors such as stone tool making.

There are a lot of species in this genera (at least 10 and maybe more!). Because of this they are often divided into two groups: the gracile and the robust. As these names imply, the robust group consist of australopithecines that have large molars, thick enamel, and show signs of sizable chewing muscles. These robust australo-pithecines are believed to have become specialized in their diets, perhaps focusing on a dietary niche of harder, more fibrous plants. This is reflected in their skeletal anatomy with many robust species having crests or ridges of bone on the top of their skulls where the chewing muscles attach. The early *Homo* species overlapped with some of the robust australopithecines and may have interacted with each other. Most anthropologists think that the origins of the genus *Homo* lie with the gracile ones, which are less-specialized in their diet.

The earliest known member of the genus is *Australopithecus anamensis*, dating from 4.2–3.8 mya. Its overall morphology is similar to *Ardipithecus*. This species is found in Kenya and Ethiopia and has a mixture of primitive traits such as large canines and a small cranium, alongside a more derived morphology in its limbs. A good hypothesis is that *Au. anamensis,* species is directly related to *Ar. ramidus*. They also share morphology with a later species, *Australopithecus afarensis*. Some scientists think *Au. anamensis* evolved into *Au. afarensis*, but there is overlap between the last known *Au. anamensis* fossils and the first appearance of *Au. afarensis*.

Australopithecus afarensis lived from 3.9 mya to 3 mya in Ethiopia and Tanzania. An adult female found in 1974 in the Hadar region of Ethiopia became world famous as it was one of the most complete fossils of a hominin ever found. Sometimes referred to by the name Lucy (after the Beatles song 'Lucy in the Sky with Diamonds'), it is also known by its Amharic name Dinkinesh, which means 'you are marvelous.' She would have been 1.2 m (3.9 ft) tall. *Au. afarensis* had a average cranial capacity of around 440 cm^3.

Interestingly, a fossil of a 3-year-old *Australopithecus afarensis* from Dikika retains the hyoid bone, a horseshoe-shaped bone found in the throat. The hyoid bone in humans is different from that of chimps, reflecting adaptations to speech. By studying this bone, we can understand something about the sounds a species could make. As the *Au. afarensis* hyoid is more similar to an ape than to humans, is suggests the species did not have language, at least not in the way humans do.

One of the most incredible finds associated with *Au. afarensis* comes from the site of Laetoli, where archaeologists discovered a series of fossilized footprints left by the species. They show that Dinkinesh's species had a big toe in line with their other toes. In other words, it was not divergent. This species used its big toe to propel itself forward in the same way many humans do today.

In southern Africa, the best-known species of australopithecines is *Australopithecus africanus*, which flourished from as early as 3.7 mya to 2.2 mya, but there has been a lot of debate as to the exact geological age of many of these fossils. They had ape-sized brains but they seem to have lost much of the adaptation to arboreal life. Some recent work suggests that they might be descendants of *Au. anamensis* but their exact ancestor is not known.

As for the robust australopithecines, compared to the gracile species they had thick, large molars and often had thick crests of bone on the top and back of their skulls for muscle attachment. The group of australopithecines put in this group include *Au. robustus* (found in south Africa), *Au. boisei* (found in east Africa), and *Au. aethiopicus* (found in east Africa). As a group, these species date from 2.5 million to 1.5 mya. It is also interesting to note that some of the best evidence for stone tool manufacture in the australopithecines comes from sites associated with these robust species sites.

For some scholars, the adaptations shared among these three species of robust australopithecines suggests that they share a similar origin. If that is true, they would consist of a mono-phylum. In that case, it would be best to put them into their own genus, *Paranthropus*. Others, however, think the similarities in the southern and eastern robust australopithecines are due to independent species finding similar solutions. In this case, both populations found a new niche to exploit and then evolved larger chewing adaptations. In other words, the similarities of *Au. robustus* and *Au. boisei* are due to homoplasy. The *Paranthropus* designation is favored by many scholars but this could change with more research.

Australopithecus sediba is known from two skeletons, MH 1 and MH 2, from a single cave site in South Africa. The species dates to 1.9 mya. Its brain size was ~ 400 cm^3, though estimates of this vary, with a stature estimate of around 1.5 m (4.9 feet). While aus-tralopithecine-like in many respects, there are also some features that are more derived, such as smaller cheek teeth and a brain that is shaped more like members of the genus *Homo*. This has led some to suggest that it is the direct ancestor of early *Homo*.

What was life like for the australopithecines? One early hypothesis suggested that they were top hunters, killing not only other mammals but each other. This theory, called the osteodontokeratic culture, saw australopithecines using horns, teeth, and bones to hunt antelope and to cannibalize other members of their species. See Chapter 7 for more about the violent and warlike origins of hominins.

However, later work showed this was wrong. Taphonomic research, the study of what happens to a bone from when an organism dies to when it is studied by a researcher, demonstrated that australopithecines were most likely the *hunted* rather than the *hunters*. The bones in the cave deposits, including those of australopithecines, were the result of accumulations by large carnivores. Still there are some indications that they had a varied diet and occasionally ate vertebrate meat.

It seems likely that during the time australopithecines lived there were multiple lineages of hominins in Africa. Australopithecines and early *Homo* likely overlapped. In fact, research at the site of Koobi Fora, Kenya shows footprints of two different sets of hominins. While it is difficult to know for sure, the excavators argue that one set was left by a larger *P. boisei* individual, while two or three smaller *Homo* species, most likely *Homo erectus*.

Overall, our knowledge of australopithecines has led to revelations of early hominin behavior. While they had small brains and small bodies, they seem to have had at least some form of culture, perhaps even making bone and stone tools.

THE GENUS *HOMO*

When the genus *Homo* first appeared is difficult to know. We tend to think that the first members of our genus would not have had very large jaw muscles and would have faces that were less prognathic than in the majority of australopithecines. We also assume that they would have larger brains, be fully bipedal, and be able to make efficient stone tools.

The earliest proposed species are *Homo habilis*, *Homo rudolfensis*, and *Homo erectus*, with the first of two of these resemble

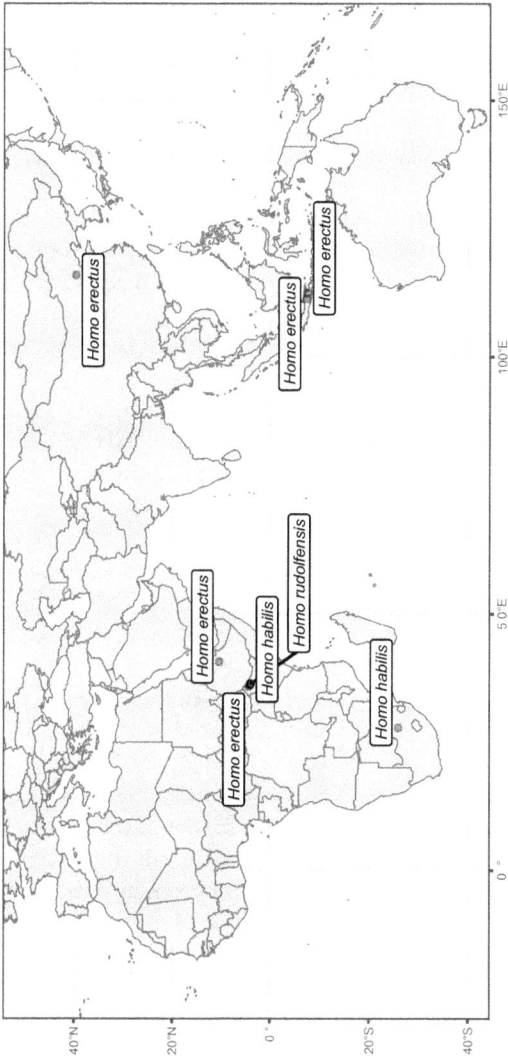

Figure 5.4 Map of some early *Homo* sites.

australopithecines more than they do later species of the genus *Homo*. Some scholars have even suggested it would be better to put these species into the Australopithecine genus instead. This suggestion has not been well-accepted, but as we will see *H. erectus* has distinctive derived traits that suggest changes to its behavior that are much more human-like.

One of the earliest plausible members of our genus is represented by a mandible from the Ledi Geraru research area, Afar Regional State, Ethiopia. Dating to between 2.8 mya and 2.75 mya, this jaw (found by Chalachew Seyoum) is from the left side of the mouth and has a mixture of australopithecine features alongside some more modern ones. The Ledi Geraru mandible is a sort of transitional fossil with some dental traits are more modern, suggesting that a derived dental anatomy was an early hallmark of the *Homo* lineage. These changes may have been accompanied by brain size expansion, technological innovations in stone tool manufacture and changes in behavior. But as of now there is no species designated for this fragmentary jaw.

Homo habilis dates from 2.8 mya to as recent as 1.5 mya and is found in east and southern Africa. It is unclear which Australopithecine species *H. habilis* descended from. While their average brain size is 630 cm³ they still are not very tall, averaging about 1 meter tall (3.2 ft), (a bit shorter than Lucy). Derived traits in this species include a brain case that is rounder than seen in most australopithecines and feet that show signs of obligate bipedalism with no grasping ability. However, they have large teeth like australopithecines and somewhat long arms.

Since they are overall fairly primitive in their skeletal morphology, why is this species put in the genus *Homo*? Historically they were seen as the first tool makers, creators of a lithic industry known as the Oldowan. The name *Homo habilis* means 'handy man.' *H. habilis* created stone tools by choosing two rocks, one that we call the hammer and one that we call the core. Oldowan tools are made by smashing the hammer tool into the core. If this is done at the right angle, a small **flake** of stone will be removed from the core. The flake can be used to cut meat off bone while the remaining core may have been used to smash open bones to access the marrow inside. While the technology is often represented as very simple, it does take some time to learn how to do this [see below for more on stone tools].

For a long time, anthropologists thought that only members of the genus *Homo* could make and use stone tools. But in 2015 scientists announced the discovery of stone tools at a site in Kenya called Lomekwi. The Lomekwian tools date to 3.3 mya. They are larger than the known Oldowan tools and the date suggests that they were made by an australopithecine species. This work supports earlier research that found evidence of tool-marks on animal bones near where the *Australopithecus garhi* skull was discovered.

Depending on what fossils are included in the group *H. habilis* shows a lot of variation in its cranium. One skull, KNM-ER 1813 dates to 1.7 mya has a 500 cm³ brain and a small, prognathic face. KNM-ER 1470 is also about 1.7 million years old and has a 750–800 cm³ brain with a large, flatter face. For some scholars these differences are extreme enough that they place KNM-ER 1813 in the *H. habilis* species and KNM-ER 1470 is in a different species called *Homo* rudolfensis. The debate centers on if KNM-ER 1813 and KNM-ER 1470 represent the variation in size exhibited by early *Homo* due to sexual dimorphism or because they are different species.

Homo erectus flourished from ~2 mya to as recently as 0.3 mya (though the last appearance date of this species is unclear). This species is often described as the first 'global' hominin, being the first of our ancestors to be found outside of Africa. Its body plan is much more human-like than anything that came before, but they still had a pronounced brow ridge and a low, flat skull. However, they had short arms and long legs, a ratio seen in *Homo sapiens* today. They reached human height and had a wide range of cranial capacities from 600 to 1,200 cm³, with the largest brained *H. erectus* approaching *H. sapiens* in brain size. There is good evidence they were eating vertebrate meat by either hunting or by scaring off predators to access their kills. There is also less sexual dimorphism seen in this species, another trait making them seem more human than previous species. The growth and development data suggest that this species grew up faster than *H. sapiens* but slower than apes. *H. erectus* colonized regions outside of Africa. As soon as we see the species in Africa we begin to see it elsewhere, such as sites in Georgia and Java.

Getting taller seems to be a trait that was selected for in *H. erectus*. One of the most amazing of *H. erectus* finds is that of Nariokotome boy, a juvenile erectine from Kenya that was ~80% complete. Scientists are not certain how tall he would have been if he became an adult, but estimates range from 1.75 meters (5.7 ft) to close to 1.9 meters (6.2 ft). A tall *H. erectus* would have been about 50% taller than an average australopithecine. To put this into perspective, a human today who 50% taller than someone who was 1.75 meters would be 2.6 meters (8.5 feet).

There is also good data to suggest that they were able to control fire. When and how hominins began to cook is a hot topic, but research suggests that by 800,000 years ago *H. erectus* populations were using fire to cook foods. While most scholars focus on the technical utilitarian reasons for fire use there may be a more nuanced and important aspect—conversation and storytelling. Polly Wiessner's study of evening campfire conversations by the Ju/'hoansi of Namibia and Botswana implies that it was during talks over firelight that humans engaged in non-subsistence related conversations that aroused the imagination; spreading rumors and spinning tales.

Another key evolutionary change that has to do with how early hominins obtained meat. There has been a lot of discussion around the question of the role of meat eating in human evolution, with some arguing that meat eating is one of the behaviors that made us human. This though might be an oversimplification. Most of the stone tools we know of at this time are not necessarily weapons. Perhaps this is part of the process of getting taller. *H. erectus* reaching human stature seems to be a significant change in their overall anatomy. It is hard to be active in the noon-day sun so sweating helps to cool us down (but only if we have no body hair). With longer legs someone can walk even farther and increase their home range in search of water, food, or sources for stone tools.

Longer limbs allow for what is called persistence hunting, where a hunter literally runs an animal to death. Since most prey cannot sweat, they get overheated if chased for a long time. Ethnographic accounts of foraging groups suggest that this method of hunting may have been common. Running adaptations such as long legs and larger semicircular canals in *H. erectus* suggest that this could have worked for them as well.

It is after the spread of *H. erectus* that the story of human evolution becomes one about the interactions between members of the genus *Homo*. As *H. erectus* adapted to new regions and developed new cultural systems, regional variants of the species appeared. Some of these versions of hominins may have adapted enough to become new species. The next chapter explores these variants. Before that, though, there are some major questions that need to be addressed.

MAJOR QUESTIONS IN EARLY HUMAN EVOLUTION

The next chapter concentrates on the question of where our species, *H. sapiens*, comes from. However, it is helpful to take a step back and consider some of the major debates in paleoanthropology and how they can help us to understand the origins of our species.

STONE TOOLS

Stone tools are one of the most ubiquitous aspects of early human culture. While nonhuman primates can use tools, manufactured lithics are, for the most part, connected to the hominin lineage. Chimpanzees will sometimes use one rock as an anvil and place a nut on top. They will then use a second rock as a hammer, smashing it against the nut to. Capuchin monkeys use a similar method, with archaeological evidence that this was practiced for thousands of years.

There is something different, though, about the way hominins began to make stone tools. To make a stone tool, a hominin uses one stone to remove a flake from another stone by smashing them together. This process, called knapping, results in the second stone (called the core) having flakes removed from it. As noted above, the current earliest direct evidence for stone tool manufacture is seen in the Lomekwian culture that dates to 3.3 mya. There is also indirect evidence, in the form of marks left by stone tools on bones, that dates to 3.6 mya.

Not all scholars accept these earlier dates, partly because they come from a small sample of sites. For that reason, many put the first stone tool tradition as the Oldowan, which appears around

2.6 mya. This consists of chopper tools and flakes and is often associated with early members of the genus *Homo*. During lithic reduction, the core tool becomes what is known as a chopper. These choppers may have been used to break open the limb bones of prey animals to access the marrow inside. Choppers were also used to work wood and other plant materials. It is likely that the flakes were also used for multiple actions, with the sharp edge of a flake can be used as a sort of 'tooth' to help remove meat from a bone.

While some early Oldowan tools seem to have been made without much forethought, as techniques became better there is some indication that the removal of flakes was done in a way to maximize production.

The second major stone tool tradition is the Acheulean, best associated with *H. erectus*. Unlike in the Oldowan, it seems the main goal was to sharpen the core tool into a specific shape, something that archaeologists call a handaxe. These tools are flaked on both sides of the core, leaving an object that is somewhat symmetrical in appearance. The exact function of these tools is unclear. Studies of the wear on the edges of these tools, plus modern recreations and experiments, suggest they were used for woodworking, digging, and butchering animal carcasses. For these reasons that they might have had multiple functions.

What has intrigued many archaeologists is the idea that the handaxe shows the transmission of more than just the idea of making stone tools, but the know-how to make them. This passing of information would be a cultural trait that shows *H. erectus* individuals passing down information in a distinctively human manner. Anthropologists have shown that areas of the brain used to create language and those used to produce tools overlap.

After the Acheulean we find many different types of stone tools associated with different groups and/or species. One of the best studied is the Mousterian tradition associated with Neandertals. Neandertals were making smaller flakes, scrapers, and points. The latter may have been hafted onto spears or other objects. To make these points, a knapper first shapes the core in a specific way so that with a final strike the flake that pops off the core is of a size and shape that they planned for. This is not easy to do and takes a lot of practice for modern day knapper to learn.

While once thought to be the purview of only members of the genus *Homo*, scholars today know that stone tool use is broader. It is also highly likely that other tools were being made and used that do not preserve. Tools made of wood, for example, are not likely to be found after millions of years. Tools made of perishable materials such as wood were probably being used at the same time or even before stone tools evolved.

BRAIN SIZE

One of the emerging patterns over the 7 million years of human evolution is encephalization, an increase in brain size over time. There are different methods used to measure the cranial capacity of a fossil. Measurements of specific landmarks on the skull can be used to extrapolate the endocranial volume of the skull. Other methods include filling a complete cranium with an object like seeds and then measuring the volume of seed. Nowadays, many scholars use a version of computed tomography to estimate the skull's volume. This measurement is often given in cubic centimeters (cm^3), which is equal to one milliliter (about 0.2 teaspoons).

As Figure 5.5 shows, there is a general pattern of larger brains over time. It is unclear if this expansion was due to gradual growth over time or instead if we are seeing the results of rapid change in brain size followed by a period of stasis. When we see periods of no change followed by these bursts, it is often referred to as punctuated equilibrium. Punctuated equilibrium suggests that populations stay the same for long periods of time and this stability is interrupted, or punctuated, by burst of rapid change. The other view, known as phyletic gradualism, sees evolution as a more gradual change over time.

Brains are expensive organs to maintain. Some estimates suggest that for the same amount of tissue, brains require more than 20 times the metabolic energy as muscle tissue does. If they are so 'expensive' why did hominins need to evolve larger brains? This question is hard to answer when we note that australopithecines and early members of the genus *Homo* seem to have been fairly successful without these large brains.

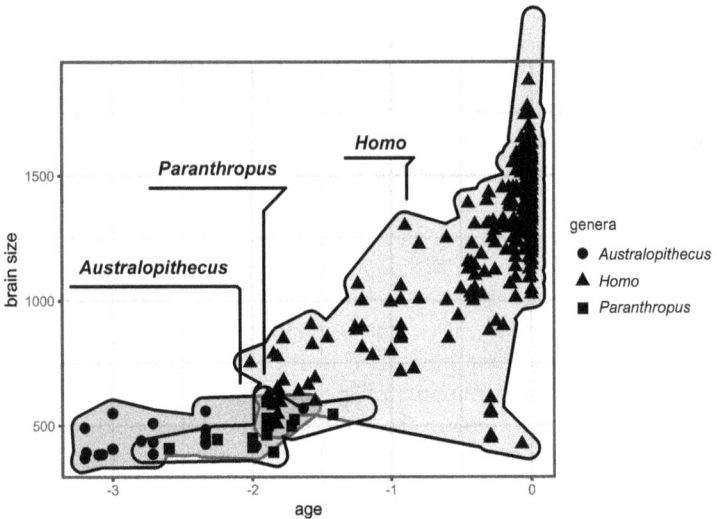

Figure 5.5 Brain size increasing over time. On the left-hand side of the graph, we see *Australopithecus* and *Paranthropus*, which have relatively small cranial capacities compared to later *Homo*. But early members of the genus *Homo* have brains similar in size to the australopithecines. It is not until *Homo erectus* appears that brain size begins to reach closer to 1,000 cm^3.

One potential answer has to do with diet. Perhaps brain size expansion is linked with a switch to a diet of vertebrate meat. Encephalization might have helped hominins solve the problems of hunting. Hominins did not have large claws or other hunting adaptations. This is important, since it is not until 300,000 years ago there is good evidence for the use of spears and hunting weapons. The archaeological record suggests that large-bodied hominins were able to access prime-aged prey. If they hunted these animals or scavenged from other predators is not known, but it does seem like they had priority access to carcasses, indicating that they were able to hunt or scare off other carnivores. This would suggest a feedback loop, where larger brains allowed for better access to meat, which in turn helped to 'fuel' those brains. Working in groups and using language and signals to plan out hunting strategies would be good adaptations to have.

CHAPTER SUMMARY

The question of why hominins evolved in the first place has been the genesis of the research covered in this section. Scientists have often looked for what they call a 'prime mover,' the main reason for something happening. Various prime movers such as language, symbolic thought, larger brains, and tool use have been proposed. But the truth of the matter is that human origin is much more complex. The next chapter brings this all together to talk about where *Homo sapiens* come from.

1. Hominins are primates that are closer to *Homo sapiens* than to any other living primate. They are our direct ancestors.
2. Hominins are recognized via two changes: a reduction in canine size (a reflection of change in diet or in social system) and signals of bipedality.
3. The earliest hominins are represented by fragmentary fossils but the data suggest that both bipedalism and small canines evolved starting between 7 mya and 6 mya.
4. Australopithecines flourished from 4 mya to 1 mya. One of these species is the ancestor of the genus *Homo* but we are not sure which one.
5. *H. erectus* is the first hominin to approach the brain size and behavioral repertoire we see in *H. sapiens*.

FURTHER READING

Barr, W. Andrew, Briana Pobiner, John Rowan, Andrew Du, and J. Tyler Faith. No Sustained Increase in Zooarchaeological Evidence for Carnivory after the Appearance of *Homo Erectus*. 2022. *Proceedings of the National Academy of Sciences* 119(5): e2115540119. https://doi.org/10.1073/pnas.2115540119. *Research by Barr and colleagues argues that there is no clear sign in an increase in carnivorous diet between 2.6 mya and 1.2 mya, which would push back on the claim that this was a time of a major change in human diet.*

Berger, Lee R., Darryl J. de Ruiter, Steven E. Churchill, Peter Schmid, Kristian J. Carlson, Paul H. G. M. Dirks, and Job M. Kibii. 2010. *Australopithecus Sediba*: A New Species of *Homo*-like Australopith from South Africa. *Science* 328(5975): 195–204. https://doi.org/10.1126/science.1184944. *The first description of Australopithecus sediba*

Brunet, Michel, Franck Guy, David Pilbeam, Daniel E Lieberman, Andossa Likius, Hassane T Mackaye, Marcia S Ponce de Leon, Christoph Zollikofer, and Patrick Vignaud. New Material of the Earliest Hominid from the Upper Miocene of Chad. *Nature* 437 (2005): 752–755. *An overview of the Sahelanthropus fossils.*

DeSilva, Jeremy. 2021. *First Steps: How Upright Walking Made Us Human.* William Collins. *Detailed overview of what we know about the evolution of upright walking and how it led to humans being a global and successful species.*

Kimbel, William H., and Lucas K. Delezene. 2009. 'Lucy' Redux: A Review of Research on *Australopithecus Afarensis. American Journal of Physical Anthropology* 140(S49): 2–48. https://doi.org/10.1002/ajpa.21183. *Science-heavy piece on* Australopithecus afarensis.

Lovejoy, C. Owen. 2009. Reexamining Human Origins in Light of *Ardipithecus Ramidus. Science* 326(5949): 74. https://doi.org/10.1126/science.1175834. *An attempt to explain the role bipedalism and low sexual dimorphism played in human origins.*

Pargeter, Justin, Cheng Liu, Megan Beney Kilgore, Aditi Majoe, and Dietrich Stout. 2023. Testing the Effect of Learning Conditions and Individual Motor/Cognitive Differences on Knapping Skill Acquisition. *Journal of Archaeological Method and Theory* 30(1): 127–171. *In-depth look at what we know about the making of stone tools.*

Schrein, Caitlin. 2015. Lucy: A Marvelous Specimen. *Nature Education Knowledge* 6(7): 2. *A good overview on Lucy.*

Stout, D., and T. Chaminade. Stone Tools, Language and the Brain in Human Evolution. *Philosophical Transactions of the Royal Society B* 367 (2012): 75–87. https://doi. org/10.1098/rstb.2011.0099. *More on stone tools and their link to language.*

Wiessner, Polly W. 2014. Embers of Society: Firelight Talk among the Ju/'hoansi Bushmen. *Proceedings of the National Academy of Sciences* 111(39): 14,027–14,035. https://doi.org/10.1073/pnas.1404212111. *An interesting take on the role of fire in human evolution.*

PALEOANTHROPOLOGY (II)

Homo sapiens

CHAPTER OVERVIEW

The only living hominin today is *Homo sapiens*. How this happened, and what connections existed between *H. sapiens* and other hominins, is the subject of this chapter. The story of human evolution after one million years ago is one of diversification of ways of being humans, followed by the spread of one population, *H. sapiens*. Recent scholarship suggests that *H. sapiens* interbred with other hominin populations. This process of gene and information exchange is what lead to the contemporary human genome.

At the end of the last chapter, *Homo erectus* had begun to spread across Africa, Europe, and Asia. As hominins reached these regions, the regional populations adapted to different ecological regions. What happened next is a question that paleoanthropologists spend a lot of time thinking about. In some instances, these populations become different species, evolving new, derived features. For example, a *Homo erectus* population reached the island of Flores in South East Asia around 1 million years ago. Once they arrived on the island (probably by boat, though we do not have any direct evidence of watercraft at this point) they adapted to the local island environment. The species, *Homo floresiensis*, became smaller, due mostly to the Island Rule discussed in Chapter 3. Nicknamed 'the Hobbits,' this group of hominins lived on the island until around 50,000 years ago, at which time they disappeared, replaced a few thousand years later by *H. sapiens*. Similar events occurred elsewhere in Eurasia and Africa. At the end of this chapter, we will see hominis as a global species, with a

DOI: 10.4324/9781003390442-7

revolutionary new way of living by growing plants and adapting to agriculture.

WHAT HAPPENED DURING THE MIDDLE PLEISTOCENE?

During the Middle Pleistocene (780,000–126,000 years ago) the amount of variation within and between hominin groups was enormous. Hominins became a colonizing species at this time and we begin to see regional differences in populations. In general we find hominins that, compared to contemporary humans, have larger faces, bigger teeth, no chins, and were overall more robust. There are also signs of more complex behaviors such as language, burial of the dead, creation of complex tools, and symbolic thought. The dispersal of hominins across Europe, Asia, and Africa means that we must reconcile the variations of types of hominins at this time.

Some of the proposed species for this time period include *Homo antecessor, Homo heidelbergensis, Homo neanderthalensis, Homo mauritanicus, Homo rhodesiensis, Homo helmei, Homo sapiens, Homo luzonensis, Homo naledi, Homo longi,* and *Homo bodoensis.* For each of these hypothesized species researchers debate which fossils to place in that species. Lumpers are paleoanthropologists who tend to put fossils into a small number of species, using more broad categories, while splitters put the same group of fossils into more distinct species. At its core, the question becomes one of how much variation we should expect to see in a species. This is not an easy question to answer. Moreover, in the last few decades the use of genetic data and ancient DNA has revolutionized how we explore species in the past.

The **Out of Africa hypothesis** suggests that contemporary humans originated in a small population in Africa and then outcompeted the other species, either directly or indirectly. This model sees ancient populations belonging to many different species and argues that there is a species-level differentiation of *H. sapiens* and Neandertals.

The **Multiregional model** hypothesizes that humans originated in more than one region. It suggests that ancient people belonged to only a few species that were connected by gene flow throughout the Middle Pleistocene. Proponents of this theory point to similarities between Neandertals and *H. sapiens* to suggest that they are all part of a larger metapopulation.

Below is an overview of a sample of the proposed species, focusing on the best-known and most-studied species.

THE NEANDERTALS

Neandertals are the best-studied and analyzed population of archaic humans. In fact, the first Neandertal fossils were uncovered *before* Darwin published his *Origin of Species*. Much has been written about their general biology and lifeways. They were first found in the Neander Valley, near Düsseldorf, Germany, which is where their name comes from. There is a bit of a debate among biological anthropologists as to the proper way to spell Neandertal, with some preferring Neanderthal. The reasons for this are due to a change in the way the German word for valley is spelled (changing from 'thal' to 'tal' in 1901). Some prefer to keep the old spelling while others prefer to use the more modern version.

Some of the most salient aspects of Neandertal morphology are found on their skulls, which are long and low. Their cranial capacity has an average of roughly 1500 cm^3. The occipital bun, a projection on the upper part of the occipital bone of the cranium, is a key Neandertal trait. Other aspects of their crania that are derived in Neandertals are their large browridge and the suprainiac fossa, a depression in the bone that is rugose and porous.

Neandertals are often described as being cold-adapted, with short and stocky bodies. A reconstructed Neandertal skeleton (based on fossils from different sites in Europe and Southwest Asia) yields a height estimate of 1.63 m (5.3 feet). Their body plan follows the predictions of Bergmann's rule (as temperature decreases body mass increases) and Allen's rule (animals in cold climates have shorter limbs than those in warmer climates). The Neandertal nose may have aided in temperature and moisture exchange, which would lower the loss of body heat during inspiration. Some have argued that they have large noses to warm and humidify the cold, dry air. Recent scholarship has questioned some of the underlying assumptions of the causes of Neandertal facial morphology, suggesting that cold adaptation may not explain classic Neandertal features such as their nasal region.

The Neandertal chest is also adapted to climatic stress. Their rib cage flares outward toward the pelvis, contrasting with modern humans who have a more 'barrel-shaped' rib cage. While this could be a cold adaptation to increase the surface area/volume ratio as predicted by Bergmann's rule, it may also be due to higher activity levels which would require greater lung capacity.

In general, the behavioral traits of Neandertals are also complex. While earlier archaeologists assumed that they were not as behaviorally complex as *Homo sapiens*, this seems to be incorrect. Neandertals uses a prepared-core technology (see Chapter 5) which allowed them to create scrapers to work hides and spear points to hunt prey. They also had control of fire, had complex mortuary rituals, engraved on rock, and maybe even made musical instruments (though all of this is debated).

In May of 2010 scientists published the first complete DNA sequence of a Neandertal genome, taken from a bone from a site in Siberia. This and subsequent work showed a number of surprising aspects of Neandertal biology. For one, Neandertals were not genetically diverse. The level of variation in their genome is less than seen in humans today, suggesting that they had a small population size. But the most celebrating aspect of the Neandertal DNA studies was that there was good evidence of interbreeding with *Homo sapiens*. Recent work suggests that there were multiple periods of inbreeding between these groups. Many people today have about 2% of their genome from Neandertals. There is also evidence that over time the percentage of Neandertal genes in humans has decreased, perhaps as natural selection weeds out deleterious mutations.

DENISOVANS

While trying to obtain more samples of ancient DNA, paleo-geneticists recovered DNA a finger bone from Denisova cave in Siberia. Expecting to find Neandertals, the DNA proved to be significantly different from both humans and Neandertals. The discovery of a hominin population in Europe that was genetically distinct from Neandertals and from contemporary humans was a big shock to paleoanthropologists.

Denisovans are a sister population of Neandertals. Comparison between these groups suggests Denisovans and Neandertals share a common history. The direct ancestors of contemporary humans separated from this lineage, which subsequently branched into Denisovans and Neandertals. Denisovans contributed genetic material to many Southeast Asian populations, including Melanesians and aboriginal Australians.

As we learn more about this species it has become clear that Denisovans were connected with other human species. In 2018 geneticists showed that a 90,000-year-old fossil was a Neandertal–Denisovan hybrid. Nicknamed Denny, she was found in the same cave as the original Denisovans sample. This 13-year-old girl had a father who was Denisovan and a mother who was a Neandertal. Even more amazing, the work shows that her Denisovan father had Neandertal DNA in him, suggesting he was the result of mixing between populations many generations before Denny was born.

Unfortunately, there are only a few fossils that have been found that might be from Denisovans. Those fossils suggest a wide ecological adaptation, from the Tibetan plateau to Siberia. One possible candidate is a jawbone that was dredged from off shoe of Taiwan, in the Penghu Channel. Dated to between 190,000 and 100,000 years ago, genetic evidence suggests this fossil was a male Denisovan.

As this book was being edited, scholars announced a spectacular new find. Fossilized plaque from the Harbin skull, a 146,000 year old cranium from China, showed that the individual had Denisovan DNA. This skull has a wide and prognathic face and a large brow ridge, resembling other fossil from the Middle Pleistocene. It had been put into the species *Homo longi*, but these new results may make anthropologists rethink its attributions.

HOMO FLORESIENSIS

In 2003, a team of researchers announced the discovery of a new species, *Homo floresiensis* on the on the island of Flores in Indonesia. Originally dated to 80,000 years ago, what shocked scholars at the time was their small body and brain size. With about fourteen different individuals discovered, these hominins averaged about 1.06 meters (3½ feet) tall and had a cranial capacity of around 425 cm³.

The question of why they were so small has received a lot of attention. Based on their age and location, the most likely ancestor of this group is *Homo erectus*. But we know that *H. erectus* were taller and had larger brains than *H. floresiensis*. Most scientists now believe that they are small due to island dwarfism (see Chapter 3 for more on this). The ancestors of *H. floresiensis* arrived on the island over 1 million years ago and slowly evolved to be smaller. There is a likelihood that *H. sapiens* would have met and interacted with this species, as stories of 'little people' are common in the region.

HOMO NALEDI

One of the more recent species to be proposed is *Homo naledi*. This species dates to between 335,000–236,000 years ago and is found at a single cave site in South Africa called Rising Star cave. They had a small cranial capacity (one-third of our size, ranging from 460 cm^3 to 600 cm^3), were less than 1.5 meters tall (5 ft), and weighed 40 kg (90 lb). Intriguingly, this species was found are in a part of the cave that is difficult to access. Archaeologists today must be experienced cavers and have small bodies to even access the space the bones are found in (The 'chute' used to access the chamber is 18 cm (7 inches) in diameter at its smallest point).

Equally surprising is that we now have close to 15 individuals represented at the site. Overall, their anatomy is a mosaic of primitive and derived features. There are aspects of the brain morphology that are very *Homo* like, especially regions associated with socio-emotional processing. Their shoulders and upper limbs seem adapted to climbing, while their hands share features that suggest the ability to grasp and make stone tools. *H. naledi* shows many human-like anatomical aspects of the hand, foot, lower limb, dentition and cranium, albeit with a brain size equal to that of australopithecines.

Due to their mixed traits, it is hard to know where to place this species in the evolutionary lineage. Its small brain and body size are suggestive of a more primitive group, but other parts of its body seem more human-like (this is especially true of hands and feet, the body parts used to interact with the world). Future work will hopeful flesh out how they are related to other hominins.

A second question is how they got to the part of the cave they are found in. Due to the difficulty of accessing this chamber, it seems unlikely that they just wandered in and got lost. Nor is there good evidence that they were victims of predators or other hominins. Some researchers have suggested there are signs of burial and mortuary practices, but many archaeologists are not convinced that the data support this hypothesis.

HOMO SAPIENS

How do the above species differ from *Homo sapiens*? Overall, our species seems to differ from earlier groups in that we are less robust overall, have larger brains, a vertical, mostly flat face, and skull that is high vaulted and globular. *H. sapiens* are also the only hominin to all have chins. Neandertals, in contrast, have skulls that, while around the same size, are more elongated. One way to think of this difference is the difference in shape between an elongated European football and a rugby ball (or, for Americans, the difference between a rounded basketball and a more elongated US football).

The earliest sample of *Homo sapiens* comes from the site of Jebel Irhoud in Morocco. The fossils from this site date to 300,000 years ago and are considered by some to be the earliest member of our genus. The skull is very human like in its overall shape, but it is more elongated, suggesting perhaps that within the *H. sapiens* lineage brain shape continued to evolve. The site of Skhul in Israel dates to 120,000 and has at least 10 individuals that look modern in their morphology.

From here it gets difficult to trace the spread of *H. sapiens* but sites such as Kent's Cavern in England (dating to 44,000 years ago) and Peçstera cu Oase, Romania (dating around 42,000 years old) are some of the best-known sites. At this time, we find European fossils that have modern features more similar to earlier Africans and West Asians than to Neandertals, suggesting that the Neandertal phenotype was being replaced by the *H. sapiens*. Interestingly, ancient DNA studies indicate that some of the initial 'modern humans' to appear in Eurasia didn't contribute appreciably to the current European gene pool. There may have been multiple events where different human groups replaced others or at least were more demographically successful.

When *H. sapiens* enter Europe, it is the start of what is sometimes called the Upper Paleolithic. While we do not know for certain if only *H. sapiens* made the Upper Paleolithic tools, this new toolkit is different from the Middle Paleolithic that is associated with the Neandertals. The Upper Paleolithic is typified by stone tools made from blades, flakes that are twice as long as they are wide. Fishhooks suggest changing diets at the time and other tools seem to have been specialized to work bone and other organic materials.

Other cultural practices of the Upper Paleolithic include the first domesticated dogs, evidence of art on cave walls, and complex burial practices. There is also a demographic shift. Not only are there more people, but humans are living longer, allowing generational passing down of information within families and communities.

It is also around this time that people first settled the Americas and Australia. Exactly when and how people got to these continents has been the source of a lot of debate in anthropology and the exact timings of these events are unknown. Part of the issues come from changing sea levels. During the last Ice Age, a lot of the sea water was locked up in glaciers. This made sea levels lower. During the Holocene, the geological period that began roughly 11,000 years ago, the climate became warmer and the glaciers began to melt. Sea levels rose, covering parts of the earth with water. Many of the sites in which people first lived in the are probably now underwater.

The peopling of Australia is complicated by issues in dating the earliest sites. Sahul was the paleocontinent that encompassed what is now Australia, Tasmania, New Guinea, and the Aru Islands. New Guinea, for example, was only separated from the Australia around 8000 years ago, when the ice sheets melted and parts of Sahul were inundated. But people have been on Sahul since before that time. One interesting site is Madjedbebe rock shelter. The artifacts at this site include grinding stones, ground ochres, reflective additives and ground-edge hatchet heads. It dates to around 65,000. This would suggest that humans built ocean worthy vessels and sailed to Sahul, moving through Indonesia at the same time as *Homo floresiensis* was on Flores.

The peopling of America is very controversial in terms of when it was first inhabited by humans. While earlier archaeologists argued that humans arrived on the continent in a single wave of migration around 15,000 years ago, genetic, fossil, and archaeological data have suggested a more complex story. Excavations at White Sands, New Mexico uncovered fossilized human footprints that date to around 21,000 years ago. As parts of the Americas were covered in ice sheets at the time, it is hard to know how they colonized these regions, but it might be that they took a coastal route along the western part of North America.

Intriguingly, it is during the Late Pleistocene that we see the extinctions of much of the Earth's megafauna. While other extinction events have occurred, this one is somewhat unique in that it was biased towards large animals, those over 44 kg (96 lb). These extinctions seem to have begun around 50,000 years ago in Sahul and in the Americas around 14,000 years ago. As these dates correlate somewhat with the appearance of humans in those regions, there has been debate about the exact cause of these extinctions. Some think that humans hunted the megafauna to extinction. This model is often used to explain the disappearance of mammoth, mastodon and other megafauna in the Americas. Critics point out there is little direct evidence to support this model, since most of the megafauna like camels and horses show no archaeological signs of being hunted. Climate change may also be a main cause of these extinctions, though that too is hard to prove.

WHY IS *HOMO SAPIENS* THE ONLY EXTANT HOMININ?

During the Middle Pleistocene there seems to have been many different hominin species, but today the only one left is *Homo sapiens*. It could be because they had more children and were more demographically successful. As *H. sapiens* mated with other populations such as Neandertals there were simply more human genes than those from other hominins. When they hybridized, the genes from other hominins were not spread as far.

One difficulty is that we do not have many fossils of early *H. sapiens* from Africa. This makes it difficult to model the expansion of the species. Moreover, we have the problem of applying the species concept to extinct hominins. Is it even valid to refer to many of the regional variants of the Middle and Late Pleistocene as different species? Given that Neandertals interbred with *H. sapiens* should they be considered to be in the same species? These are the kinds of questions that paleoanthropologists are currently thinking about.

One field of research looks at the cognitive capabilities of *H. sapiens*. There might have been something distinctive about how *H. sapiens* think and reason. This theory, sometimes called modern human behavior, argues that *H. sapiens* were the first hominin to be able to think in a modern, contemporary way. Specifically, it is argued that we are unique in our capacity for symbolic thought. This ability allowed our ancestors to flourish and adapt to many different environments and situations.

In **semiotics**, the study of signs, there are three ways a sign is related to its subject: iconic, indexical, and symbolic. A sign is **iconic** when it resembles or looks like the object it represents. An icon has a physical resemblance to the idea or object it signifies. For example, a sketch of a bicycle on a fence may indicate that this is a bike path. An **index** signifies by causal link; there is a relationship between the sign and its object, a direct connection between the sign and its object. Smoke, for example, is an index of fire and footprints in the sand are an index that someone recently walked on the beach.

A **symbol**, however, is linked to its signifier solely by convention. People agree that the link exists but there is no direct resemblance or physical link between the sign and the object it stands for. For example, a red light means to stop but there is no causal reason for this. It just is accepted by everyone who is driving their cars. Language is one of the best examples of symbolic thought, since for most words there is no reason why they stand for the object they refer to.

Most humans are able to think symbolically. But it seems like nonhuman primates cannot. Because of this, discerning when this ability evolved in the human lineage has been of prime importance. While the fossil record suggested our species evolved 300,000 years ago, some of the archaeological evidence does not seem to show humans acting in a 'modern' way, producing art and complex technologies, until much more recently. Archaeologists recognize such behaviors by looking for signals of symbolic thought such as ornamentation, mortuary behavior, ochre use, and the production of non-utilitarian objects such as engraved objects.

At its heart, this approach is predicated on the idea that there is a clear, and archaeologically visible, dividing line between humans who act in a contemporary way and those who do not. Humans thinking in new, cognitively complex way were able to outcompete other populations or species. Scholars have tried to use the archaeological record to pinpoint exactly when humans evolved the ability to link a sign to the object it stands for simply because everyone agrees the connection exists.

The use of red ocher as a coloring agent has been suggested to be symbolic. Interestingly the earliest use dates to around 330,000 years ago, though a more intense use is seen from 160,000 to 40,000 years ago by both *H. sapiens* and Neandertals. Ancient beads might be signs of symbolic thinking since they could indicate a desire to express who you are. Beads are seen as markers of group identity and indicate the desire to let someone else know who you are (e.g., 'I'm from the group down by the river who wear necklaces pendants made from red-tinted shells and fox canines'). The act of creating beads indicates awareness of the importance of social networks. Again, the earliest proposed examples are around 300,000 years old, but these are not accepted by all archeologists. At Blombos Cave in South Africa, archaeologists have identified a change in the way beadwork was created over time and interpreted this as a reflection of changes in the social norms shared by members of a Middle Stone Age community 75,000 years ago.

For much of the intellectual history of archaeology and paleo-anthropology, the material and fossil records were viewed through a Eurocentric mindset that assumed linear progression. And over the last few decades researchers have shown that other species were engaged in behaviors that we used to think only humans could do. Neandertals have been shown to make art, engrave objects, and create jewelry. Excavations in Indonesia have uncovered examples of *Homo erectus* engraving lines on mussel shells. This artifact dates to between 540,000 and 430,000 years ago, and was engraved with a sharp object in a zigzag pattern. But, not surprisingly, claims of symbolic artifacts made by non-modern humans have been met with intense scrutiny.

This short overview of some of the species that lived during the Middle and Late Pleistocene demonstrates that there was a lot of diversity. It might be that some of these, such as *H. floresiensis*, did not contribute to the contemporary human genome. Others, like Neandertals and Denisovans, clearly did. The realization that humans today are the result of multiple periods of gene flow and hybridization from different species is a very profound one. It also has led many to question how we think about human evolution.

Now that we have a good understanding of just how diverse the genus *Homo* is we can appreciate the complexity of answering where our species came from. As noted in this chapter, ancient DNA results have shown that inbreeding between groups/species was far more common than was once believed. Additionally, fossils and archaeological evidence also suggest that hybridization was common. What this means is that today we are moving away from thinking about human evolution as if it consisted of the linear progression of humans in a tree-like system. Rather, scholars think of it more like a braided stream, in which rivers split into their own paths and then rejoin each other. While tree branches do not reconnect after they split, the different paths a river takes can and often do (see Figure 6.1).

WHAT HAPPENED AFTER THE ORIGINAL EVOLUTION OF *HOMO SAPIENS*?

For over 99% of hominin history, our ancestors were foragers, relaying on gathering and hunting to obtain enough calories to survive. While they had wide and varied diets, no one grew their own food. Instead, hominins had to hunt game and gather plants, honey, and other food to survive. This all changed with the beginning of the **Neolithic**, the 'new stone age,' when humans began to domesticate plants and animals. The one exception to this might be dogs, that could have been domesticated before this time.

The origins of agriculture is one of the major transitions in human history. As with other major transitions such as bipedalism, it had major effects on how we live, on our biology and on our culture. Starting sometime around 12,000–10,000 years ago, during the early Holocene, humans began to domesticate plants

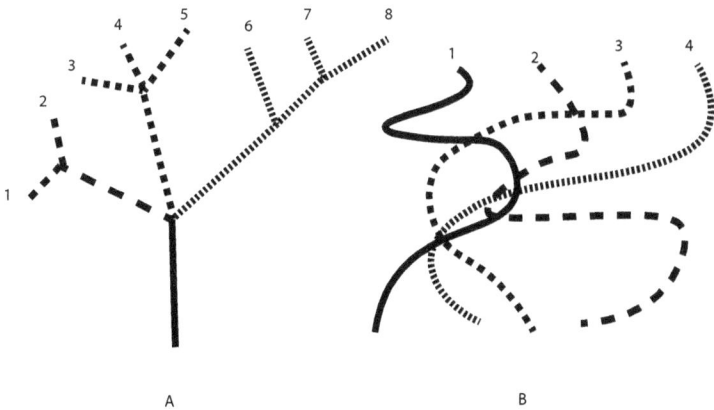

Figure 6.1 Image comparing a tree-like depiction of evolution compared to that of a braided stream. The image on the left shows a traditional species tree with roots and branches that do not overlap. The image on the right shows a braided stream model, which visualizes a more nuanced view of evolution where a species has its own evolutionary history, but may intersect and interact with each other, exchanging genes and ideas.

and animals to use as food sources. This happened independently in various parts of the world, such as in North Africa, Central America, Northeastern North America, China, and the Middle East. In fact, there might have been a dozen or so independent centers of domestication. From there, the idea of farming spread to other parts of the world. Today most humans rely on domesticated species and the few remaining foraging groups are often treated very poorly by local governments.

While documenting everything that happened during the agricultural revolution is beyond the scope of this text there are some important aspects to keep in mind for human biology. The agricultural revolution led to many changes in how humans and other species live.

Living close to animals opened humans to spread of new diseases, which lead to unprecedented mortality as people crowded together, allowing viruses and bacteria to spread easier and quickly. Agriculture also allows for large population growth. As farming spread and villages grew, more people lived in permanent settlements. This both effects the spread of disease but also the spread of ideas, genes, and culture. Farming increased the rates of sedentism as farmers tend to stay in one place due to the needs to tend to their crops and animals. This changes how people interact with each other and creates more of the need to defend your land from outsiders.

Eating new foods also changed our biology. As people began to eat softer foods, their jaw muscles became weaker since the stress on their jaws was reduced. This led to smaller mouths overall. But not to a reduction in the number of teeth we have. In other words, our mouths got smaller but our teeth did not. Overbites and underbites today are the result of this change in diet.

Switching to farming also increases the predictability of food sources. This resource predictability may have led to an increase in adult lifespan. Farming also eventually allows for the evolution of urban centers. The growth of large population centers then leads to a differentiation of social functions, creating craft specialists and other roles.

While there are many benefits, there are also some drawbacks. Almost everywhere we look, health declines overall between foraging populations and early farmers. For example, individuals from the framing villages were an average of 1.5 inches shorter than previous foragers. There are also more signs of dental caries, infections of the teeth. This is probably due to the new diet that was high in carbohydrates. Other signals include dental hypoplasia, a sign that the individual went through a stressful time and their body responded by not growing enamel in order to put energy into maintenance. Such hypoplasia is more common in agricultural societies than in hunter–gatherer populations.

Why did people adopt an economic system that led to worse overall health? From an evolutionary perspective, it might be that their health was worse, but they had a higher inclusive fitness. Farmers tend to have more children than foragers, have a short interval between births, and do not breastfeed as long. The genes of these early farmers could have spread quicker and further despite their health being worse.

No matter why it happened, it is hard to overstate the impact farming had on the human history. It allowed people to have more kids and support a larger population. As farmers spread across the world, we see their genes becoming more common, with hunter–gatherers being replaced by farming communities. It is not clear why in some parts of the world foragers switched economic systems and became farmers, while in other places these groups were outcompeted and replaced by incoming agricultural societies. Perhaps cultural and language differences influenced who became a farmer and who did not. But we know that much of human history would be quite different without domestication.

Cites, states, nations, and countries would probably not exist if it was not for agriculture. Without the excess food that farming produces it would be difficult to sustain large populations. Moreover, as note above, an economic system based on agriculture allows for a community in which not everyone is involved in food production. This, in turn, lets there be a greater number of craft specialists and for the evolution of more complex systems.

We cannot rewind the tape to see what would have happened in the absence of domestication. While it is likely that humans would still be around, the ways in which we live would be remarkably different.

CHAPTER SUMMARY

Genetic exchanges with other lineages seem to have been very common in human history. This is not surprising. Hybridization is fairly common in other species as well. Work by Rebecca Ackermann and colleagues has shown that hybrids introduce new variation into and can speed up evolution. Gene flow between distinct lineages such as Neandertals, Denisovans, early members of *H. sapiens* was probably the norm. As *H. sapiens* spread into regions that had other hominins it seems increasingly likely that inbreeding and exchange of ideas and cultures was more common than once thought.

1. There were multiple hominin species during the Middle and Late Pleistocene. The relationship between these groups is unclear, but there is evidence that many of them were interbreeding and exchanging genetic material. Human evolution is better seen as a braided stream than a tree.

2. Today the only living hominin is *Homo sapiens*. The spread of our species over the last 300,000 years may be due to a host of factors, but we also know that humans interbred with other populations.
3. Farming changed much about how we live and what our bodies look like. Without it, human history would be very different.

FURTHER READING

Ackermann, Rebecca Rogers, Alex Mackay, and Michael L. Arnold. 2016. The Hybrid Origin of 'Modern' Humans. *Evolutionary Biology* 43, no. 1 (): 1–11. https://doi.org/10.1007/s11692-015-9348-1. *A good overview of where Homo sapiens came from, looking at the plethora of data that support humans as a hybrid species.*

Baab, Karen L. 2016. The Place of *Homo Floresiensis* in Human Evolution. *Journal of Anthropological Sciences* 94: 5–18. https://doi.org/10.4436/jass .94024. *Overview of what is known about Homo floresiensis, the so-called Hobbits.*

Berger, Lee R., John Hawks, Paul H. G. M. Dirks, Marina Elliott, and Eric M. Roberts. 2017. *Homo Naledi* and Pleistocene Hominin Evolution in Subequatorial Africa. *Elife* 6: e24234. https://doi.org/10.7554/eLife .24234. *Detailed description of Homo naledi.*

Green, R. E., J. Krause, a. W. Briggs, T. Maricic, U. Stenzel, M. Kircher, N. Patterson, et al. 2010. A Draft Sequence of the Neandertal Genome. *Science* 328(5979): 710–722. https://doi.org/10. 1126/science.1188021. *While technical, this publication is the first major paper talking about the Neandertal genome.*

Sawyer, G. J., and Blaine Maley. 2005. Neanderthal Reconstructed: Anatomical Record, Part B. *New Anatomist* 283(1): 23–31. https://doi.org /10.1002/ar.b.20057. *A good overview of the biology of Neandertals.*

Vanhaeren, Marian, Francesco D'Errico, Karen L. van Niekerk, Christopher S. Henshilwood, and Rudolph M. Erasmus. 2013. Thinking Strings: Additional Evidence for Personal Ornament Use in the Middle Stone Age at Blombos Cave, South Africa. *Journal of Human Evolution* 64(6): 500–517. https://doi.org/10.1016/j.jhevol.2013.02.001. *Archaeological insight into the use of beads as personal ornaments.*

Wynn, Thomas, and Frederick L. Coolidge. 2011. *How To Think Like a Neandertal.* Oxford University Press. *Cognitive archaeologists examine what life was like for Neandertals.*

7

CONCLUSION

CHAPTER OVERVIEW

One of the lessons of twenty-first-century bioanthropology has been that many of the assumptions we have had about human biological variation and human evolution were wrong. Concepts such biological race do not accurately explain human variation. We also know *Homo sapiens* are the result of multiple species interbreeding. In this final chapter we look at some of the questions that biological anthropologists are currently debating and how the information covered in the previous chapters can help us to understand these debates.

THE SPECIES QUESTION

As discussed in Chapter 2, there are many different definitions of species. Table 7.1 provides a reminder of a few of the different species concepts.

The process for assigning a hominin to a species is a statistical one, based on the fossil's morphological measurements, its geographic location, and its geological age. But the amount of variation expected/allowed within a species is not clear. Neandertals are less varied in their morphology than contemporary humans. *Homo naledi* shows very little variation, though it should be remembered that this species is only known from a single site. Other species like *Au. afarensis* have a wide variation in size, perhaps due to sexual dimorphism. If we found two fossils in the same general region and age but one was much more robust, does that mean that we were seeing species-level differences or sexual

DOI: 10.4324/9781003390442-8

TABLE 7.1 Some of the proposed definitions of a species.

Species concept	Definition/function
Biological species concept	Defines a species as a group of organisms that have actually or could potentially interbreed in nature
Morphological species concept	Determines species solely on how similarly a group of organism looks—based entirely on physical morphology
Evolutionary species concept	A single lineage of ancestors and descendant populations which maintains its identity from other lineages in both space and time and has its own evolutionary tendencies and fate
Ecological species concept	Defines a species as a lineage which share a unique adaptive environment

dimorphism? These questions have no clear answer and often depend on looking at extant species in order to judge levels of within-species variation.

The second issue is how ancient DNA has upended what we know about species in the past. Under the biological species concept, a species is a group of organisms that have actually or could potentially interbreed in nature. In that definition, then, Neandertals and *Homo sapiens* are the same species. In that case, we might choose to refer to both as human, but that can cause confusion as well. Recent genetic studies are showing that gene flow between species, called introgression, may be more common than once thought.

For some paleoanthropologists, the opportunity to name a new species is a highlight of their professional careers. As one can imagine, identifying a fossil as a new hominin species is complicated. The International Code of Zoological Nomenclature (ICZN) is a series of conventions that most scientists follow in terms of how to name new species, which aims for continuity in the naming of species. Earlier hominin species were named after specific people (such as the person funding the work) but this practice has been mostly ended. This was ended because there are problems with naming a fossil after a person. Once a species is named the ICZN rules make it very hard to change the name, leaving us with a cave beetle with the name *Anophthalmus hitleri*. Today, scholars prefer to use a name that reflect the region and cultural heritage of where the fossil was found.

FORENSIC ANTHROPOLOGY

Lessons learned from modern forensic cases can also be applied to ancient examples. One of the most famous of these is Ötzi, a frozen body discovered in 1991 in near the Austrian-Italian border in the Alps. While originally thought to be a recent accident, the materials found with him, such as a copper axe, made the examiners question his age. Radiocarbon dating of the body showed he was 5,000 years old, having died around 3300 BCE!

Also known as the Ice Mummy, Ötzi was incredibly well preserved. He was around 45 years old when he died, 1.65 m tall (~5.4 feet) and 50 kg (110 lb). Studies of his body showed he had many tattoos and his last meal may have been red deer meat. The items found near him included the axe, some arrows, bowstring, and a pouch with flint tools and perhaps medical supplies. Scientists also recovered some of this clothing, such as his cape, coat, belt, leggings, loincloth, shoes, and cap. For a long time, scholars thought he may haven been caught in a winter storm and died. But then a study of his x-rays showed that there was an arrowhead embedded in his shoulder blade, suggesting he was shot.

Another example comes from a body discovered in a peat bog at Lindow on August 1, 1984 in Cheshire, England. When the body, sometimes known as Lindow Man or Pete Marsh, was found, it was believed to have been the remains of a recent murder victim. But analysis of the body and eventual dating showed that the individual died 2,000 years ago (50–100 CE). Lindow Man was 25–30 years old, and well-nourished and seemingly healthy at time of death. Interestingly, his last meal seems to have been a sort of bread, though chemical analysis showed that parts of the bread were burnt.

As with Ötzi, there is a lot to be said for how he died. There were lacerations over his head, a sinew loop around neck, and he had been dropped face first into a pool of water, before being placed in the bog itself. Due to this odd 'triple death' some folklorists have suggested this was a ritual death, with the individual being sacrificed. Perhaps the burnt bread piece was the remnants of how he was chosen to be sacrificed, sort of how some people today will choose the person who need to do some unpleasant task by picking the short straw.

Forensic anthropology is also used for legal issues today. This kind of work requires anthropologists to work with non-governmental organizations, victims' rights organizations, and tribunals to help investigate crimes against humanity. Humanitarian forensics consists of identifying bodies, determining causes of death, and repatriating/reburying the victims in a humane manner.

A recent example of using forensic anthropology to help social justice comes from Canada, where anthropologists have helped Indigenous communities identify the unmarked graves and bodies of young children who were taken from their homes, placed in boarding schools, and forced to stop speaking their native language. Some estimates suggest 150,000 kids went through these residential schools, which banned them from use of their cultural practices. There are estimates that more than 10,000 young people died while in the system. Anthropologists have used their skills at finding ancient graves to help locate the burial plots with ground penetrating radar to help committees working towards reconciliation.

EUGENICS

Eugenics, the self-direction of human evolution, was an integral part of genetics in the late nineteenth and early twentieth centuries. The term was coined by Francis Galton (1822–1911) and became very popular in the United States in the 1900s. At its core, eugenics is based on the idea that the human species can be improved by preventing people with 'defects' from reproducing.

Eugenicists argued that people with bad genes were outbreeding those with good genes. This, they believed, would lead to catastrophe for our species. Instead of seeing poverty as a failing of society, eugenics saw the poor as failing society by making it worse. It is important to recognize not only what the eugenicists argued but how popular it was, with many scientists and politicians supporting it. They thought they could rid the world of criminals and increase the overall intelligence of humans by sterilizing those they deemed unfit. The social Darwinists of the early twentieth century believed that the rich struggled to make it to the top and they deserve to be there. Because of this they thought the government should not pass laws to regulate their work, as society was said to advance though their work. Eugenics, however, was concerned because they thought the poor were having too many children. Under eugenics, people were poor because they were inferior. Some of the same people who were Social Darwinists were then arguing that the government *should* intervene and prevent certain people from having children, such as people who were alcoholics or unemployed.

Americans like Charles Davenport (1866–1944), Harry Laughlin (1880–1943), and Madison Grant (1865–1937) argued that the only way to prevent society from crumbling was to prevent people with 'bad genes' from entering the country and reproducing. At State Fairs in the 1920s, people could enter what were called Fitter Families Contests, where you would submit information about you and your family, have measurements taken and medical and psychological exams performed, and then be graded. If you received a B+ or higher, you would be given a certificate or coin that read 'Yea, I have a goodly heritage.' Thanks to my friend the anthropologist Jon Marks, who was able to acquire a collection of eugenics materials, I have one of these coins. Since I'm Jewish I would never have been able to get one at those contests, so I'm kinda amused to have one now …

Davenport and others wanted to institutionalize eugenics in order to keep 'defectives' out of the country via immigration laws. Laughlin's testimony to US Congress helped draft the US immigration laws in the 1920s that were the most stringent US immigration policy up to that time, reduced immigrating to US by over 90%. It was these laws that prevented many Jews from leaving Nazi Germany. Tellingly, the Nazi party used some of this work when crafting their own laws.

This work led to the infamous Supreme Court decision in *Buck v. Bell* (1927) that legalized compulsory sterilization for people deemed unfit. Coerced sterilization occurred in at least 32 states, with federally funded sterilization programs taking place throughout the twentieth century. These forced sterilizations were often done without the women's knowledge or consent, with forced sterilization of Native Americans persisting into the 1970s and 1980s.

It was not until after World War II that most Americans began to question many of these practices. The rationale for eugenics become more about saying someone is not fit to be a parent. Eugenicists stopped talked about heredity defects and rather argued the state should use its power to limit people they thought were an economic burden.

It is sometimes suggested that eugenics is a thing of the past. But in my home state of North Carolina, some estimates have 7,600 people sterilized, some of whom are still alive today. And these ideas still pop up in public discourse.

It is important to remember that genetics does not work the way eugenicists thought. There are no genes for feeblemindedness. Scientists of the 1920s were very supportive of eugenics, however. For this reason, it is always important to remember that when scientific ideas seem to be on one side and human rights are on the other, we need to be careful and think deeply.

The same is true of other attempts to use genetics to explain patterns that could be better explained by social inequality. The slavery hypertension hypothesis is a good example of this type of thinking. This theory argues that the reason that Black Americans have high hypertension has to do with events during the slave trade between 1500 and the 1860s. There is little support for it. Dehydration and salt depletion were not major causes of death on slave ships. And ancestral populations in west Africa do not seem to have high hypertension. Instead, it is more likely that racism is at the root of these health disparities.

Today, scientific racism continues to misuse science to promote ideas that races are hierarchical and immutable. But these studies begin with a set of conclusions that races can be ranked by biological criteria, a conclusion we know to be false.

Eugenicists worked by gathering 'facts' to support conclusions, then citing these ideas as proof that the original conclusions were true. As Angela Saini points out in *Superior*, her book on race science, oppression of populations has often been rationalized through the idea that inequality is a natural product of human biological difference. Anthropology has shown that when people in power make value judgements about what traits are acceptable and good, and which traits are undesirable and bad, this rarely ends well. But we also cannot separate the history of eugenics from the history of anthropology.

HUMAN IMPACTS

The Anthropocene is a proposed geological time period that reflects the time during which humans began to impact the planet, used to emphasize the impact of human activity in transforming the Earth. It is likely that humans have impacted the Earth for a long time, though the extent of this impact is unclear, and the terminology here is often seen to reflect the impact human activity has had on the climate, loss of biodiversity, and changes in the chemical makeup of the Earth. While there is no one accepted start date for this epoch, various dates such as the extinction of megafauna around 13,000 years ago, the start of the Industrial Revolution or the mid-twentieth century have been proposed. Some scholars have even proposed that embracing the term Capitalocene, which looks at the impact capitalism has had on the climate. How climate change is impacting humans and other animals today is of immense concern to many scientists. Changes in ocean temperature and costal erosion are already producing changes in how many people live and work.

Recent work has shown human activity is driving the evolution of other species. A study of the craniums of rodent species in Chicago showed that eastern chipmunks have been affected by urbanization. A decrease in their toothrow length may reflect a dietary shift, as the chipmunks no longer needed larger teeth to access nuts since they could rely on the food humans left behind. A similar impact was seen in cod, where there has been an almost 50% reduction in body size of these fish from 1996 to 2019 due to anthropogenic pressures. Commercial fishing uses large nets to capture cod. The smaller cod can swim through the nets, allowing them to survive. Genomic studies of the fish point to non-random changes occurring, suggesting that a form of human-induced selection is occurring.

Similarly, it is not uncommon to read or hear that humans have stopped evolving. This is often argued to be the result of our complex culture reducing the effect that the environment has on us.

But as discussed throughout, evolution is more than just adapting to the environment. Mutations, recombination, and gene flow won't stop. Nor will genetic drift, which will continue to effect populations.

Gene flow has increasing over the last few centuries. This is especially true when we look at the effects of globalization, the spread and connectedness of production, distribution, consumption, communication, and technologies across the world. Globalization leads to the exchange of ideas, products, cultures worldwide. And with this comes people's alleles. The ability to travel also has influenced human evolution. In the 1800s it took two months to cross the Atlantic by ship while today one can fly across the ocean in a few hours by plane. Only a few thousand years ago it would be very difficult to have objects that were made from materials more than 100 miles away. And if you did have something that came from far away you would have been among the elite. Today, few humans own things made only in their home country.

There are also more people on the planet now than there was 10,000 years ago. This means that there are more mutations. A good example of this is the spread of lactase persistence. Before the agricultural revolution almost no human adult could drink milk post-weaning without getting very sick. Now, many adults enjoy milk and other dairy products.

While the effects of natural selection might be different on a hyper-cultural species such as ourselves, we know that evolution will not stop. It is, though, hard to know what the future will hold. Biological anthropologists spend most of our time worrying about what happened in the past, but what can we say about the future of evolution? What will humans look like in the future? When asked what humans will be like 500,000 years in the future many students feel it unlikely that our species will last that long. Given what we know about human evolution, there are some reasons this might be a popular idea. Many hominin species lived for roughly 1 million years or so before going extinct or being replaced, outcompeted, or incorporated into another species. But humans today are remarkably resilient.

Others point to recent technological advances that suggest that humans in the future will incorporate computer and other technologies into their bodies as a way to enhance biological traits and go beyond the constraints of our bodies. **Transhumanism** sees technology as being used to improve our lives, perhaps by extending the human lifespan.

There is also a large ethical debate on the use of genetic engineering in humans. So-called designer babies are seen as the next frontier, where parents will be able to choose specific genes they wish their children to possess. But the likelihood that these technologies will work is unclear. We know that there are many genes that influence simple traits such as eye color so the ability to select for even more complex traits like intelligence, height, or athletic ability seems to be far away. And who has access to these technologies is also complex. If we could edit genomes, would only the super-rich be able to afford to do so? And how would that affect the already large wealth gaps? Such questions have no easy answers, but anthropological insight will have to be a major part of these discussions.

VIOLENCE

However repugnant and awful it is, warfare seems to be a fact of life for contemporary humans. When war began, then, has received a lot of attention from anthropologists. Some, like Margaret Mead who we met in Chapter 1, saw warfare as a human invention. Others see it as something deeply innate. It has even proven difficult to define warfare. One definition could be organized aggression and violence between socially distinct and autonomous groups of individuals, but whether that fits every situation is unclear. To study the origins of war, we can use archaeology to look for fortifications and weapons; bioarchaeology to search for signs of interpersonal violence; primatology, to examine claims of war occurring in nonhuman primates; and ethnography, to search for clues as to the different ways war has occurred in the past.

Some anthropologists have argued that warfare evolved out of innate tendencies for violence. In this view culture, reason, and laws are the main practices that keep humans from always fighting with their neighbors. Other scholars argue that, rather than being innate, warfare is the result of humans living in groups. For these anthropologists, war is the result of state-level societies.

The problem is that researchers do not know exactly when warfare first began. Some of the best earliest evidence comes from about 10,000–13,000 years ago. At Jebel Sahaba, a site located along the Nile River in Sudan that is estimated to be 13,000 years old. Archaeologists uncovered a cemetery that contained approximately 60 people, many of whom suffered traumatic death. At a 10,000-year-old site in Kenya called Nataruk, scientists excavated a group of people who all showed signs of violent death. One person's cranium even had an obsidian blade embedded in it.

Proponents of a long timescale for human violence often point to these sites to suggest that humans are innately violent. 45% of the individuals at Jebel Sahaba show signs of traumatic death. Taphonomic indicators of violent death in the form of arrow impacts suggest that individuals succumbed to attacks from archers. There are also healed injuries on the bones from the site, which may suggest sustained violence over an individual's lifetime.

As compelling as these cases might be, there are some important points to keep in mind. For instance, while the artifacts at Jebel Sahaba that are found associated with the bodies are often referred to as arrowheads, they could also be microliths that were attached to shafts. There is also debate about if the cemetery was the result of a onetime event or if it was used over time and thus represents different events rather than a single battle.

And even if these sites are indicators of warfare, while these examples may seem ancient, they aren't that old compared to the entire history of the genus *Homo*, which as we know evolved as early as 2.8 million years ago.

Warfare may have emerged gradually over time and evolved in concert with complex cognition. These cognitive abilities allowed humans to think well beyond the immediate moment—to communicate in new ways and to plan for future action. Complex cognition meant that humans could produce more food and trade ideas across great distances. It also allowed for the emergence of organized violence on a larger scale. A combination of symbolic thinking and complex communication allowed people to cooperate in unprecedentedly sophisticated ways, which in turn opened the door for novel forms of organized violence. Human culture provides a way for humans to wage war and justify it. (Other species, as far as we can tell, do not fight over ideas, concepts, and beliefs.)

The question of warfare's origins is important since it is are part of the larger debate about whether humans are naturally peaceful or naturally violent. Whether we are evolved to be aggressive or evolved for peace and compassion has been one of the perennial debates in bioanthropology. As we know, chimpanzees are quite violent, which might make us think our evolutionary history supports the theory that humans are evolved to fight. But at the same time, we know that bonobos are more peaceful.

The theory that humans are prone to violence was popularized in the twentieth century by journalist Robert Ardrey (1908–1980). Ardrey was a screenwriter (at one point even nominated for an Academy Award!) and was successful until the Red Scare/McCarthyism made him doubt his job prospects. Pivoting from his undergrad degree in anthropology he became a journalist. At one point, he was recommended to go to South Africa to meet with Raymond Dart, the paleoanthropologist who named *Australopithecus africanus.* At the time, Dart was having a hard time convincing his colleagues that australopithecines had culture. Ardery, however, thought Dart was right and then spent much of his time debating these ideas, popularizing the theory that humankind was born in violence. While few read his writings today, his influence has extended far beyond his books. If you have ever seen *2001: A Space Odyssey*, the opening scene of the ape-like creatures using bones to drive away others and establish dominance was inspired by Ardey's work.

On the other side of the debate was anthropologist Ashely Montagu (1905–1999). He thought that our biology was rooted in human cooperation. His books in the 1960s were often in response to Ardrey, with whom he quarreled about the innate nature of humans. While it is always tricky to sum up a scholars work in a few sentences, Montagu's general belief was that love, rather than aggression, was the thing that made us human. So, he looked towards evidence of compassion and human kindness.

The truth is probably somewhere in the middle. We are not innately warlike or innately peaceful because human culture is more complex than that. One theme of anthropology is that we need to learn to think in evolutionary terms when searching for explanations, but that we also need to keep in mind the role of human culture. The combination of anthropological findings to date would suggest that war is an aspect of a distinctively human niche that has its origins within our evolutionary history.

CONCLUSION

In 1976, anthropologist Ashely Montagu wrote that 'It is essential that we not base our image of ourselves on false foundations.' In the preface of this book, the claim was made that what makes us human is our shared evolutionary history. The chapters that followed tried to prove that by evaluating what makes humans distinctive. Everyone reading this shares an ancestry that goes back at least 7–6 million years. Knowing the processes that led to contemporary human allows us to see how similar we all are to each other. Our genetic diversity is fairly low compared to the apes, even though there are many more humans than there are chimps, gorillas, orangutans or gibbons.

Humans are biocultural, with our biology and culture interacting in complex ways. Because of this, it is hard, and often impossible, to ask which of our behaviors are nature and which are nurture. Bioanthropology can help us to better understand where we fit in the natural world as well as understand the causes and consequences of human variation. It is a fast changing and every evolving field, where we continue to find new fossils, discover new primate behaviors, and learn more about how we became human.

FURTHER READING

Austen, Ian. 2021. How Thousands of Indigenous Children Vanished in Canada. *The New York Times*, June 7, 2021. www.nytimes.com/2021/06/07/world/canada/mass-graves-residential-schools.html. *A news report on what happened to Indigenous children taken from their homes by the Canadian government.*

Chua, Liana, and Hannah Fair. 2019. Anthropocene. In *Cambridge Encyclopedia of Anthropology*, edited by Felix Stein. https://doi.org/10

"For decades, Lacan's thought is proclaimed dead, outmoded by cognitive brain sciences or by 'non-binary' (trans, LGBT+) theories of sexuality – however, Lacan's theory simply refuses to die, haunting the entire humanities as an 'undead' creature. Is it possible to resume his writings which are proverbially ambiguous and unreadable? No, it's not possible – but in his *Jacques Lacan: the Basics*, Calum Neill does the impossible. Everyone can read and understand his book: it is like a top-quality trampoline, providing a firm basis on which each of us can do all the jumps and spins we want. So from now on there are no excuses permitted to those who continue to reject Lacan's theory as an unreadable mess – we should just simply respond them: 'But did you read Calum's book?' I have no doubts that thousands will."

Slavoj Žižek, *International Director of the Birkbeck Institute for the Humanities, Global Distinguished Professor of German at New York University, Professor of Philosophy at The European Graduate School and Senior Researcher at the Institute for Sociology and Philosophy at the University of Ljubljana.*

"This foundational text teaches us about Lacan in such a way as to also make clear that 'basic' need not simplify; this is an absorbing introduction that gives us something new while outlining what we need to know if we are to take next steps into Lacanian psychoanalysis."

Ian Parker, *Secretary, Manchester Psychoanalytic Matrix*

"Countless students and colleagues have asked for a guide to all things Lacan and beyond over the years. This is the book to recommend. While Lacan was wilfully difficult, he was not immune to moments of extraordinarily concision and clarity. Neill's introduction is a wonderfully effortless read. Lacan, in my mind, would have approved of this line thrown to open hands."

Jamieson Webster, *PhD Psychoanalyst and Clinical Psychologist*

"Calum Neill's introduction to the thought of Jacques Lacan is the only introduction that will ever be necessary. Written in the most welcoming and accessible manner, this book takes us on a journey into Lacan's theory with clear explanations and vibrant examples. Neill covers all the key points while providing enough depth that one can almost feel like an expert just after reading his work. This is *the* book to get before tackling Lacan or even instead of tackling Lacan."

Todd McGowan, *Professor of Film Studies, University of Vermont*

"An indispensable and much awaited guide for those wishing to find a way into the notoriously difficult oeuvre of Jacques Lacan. Dispelling the myths whilst staying true to the radical and challenging nature of his teaching, this book provides the tools needed to discover the relentlessly captivating and ever evolving world of Lacanian thought."

Isabel Millar, *Associate Researcher, Newcastle University*